shooting the rapids in a wooden canoe

REALLIFE**STUFF**FOR**COUPLES** ON **NAVIGATING TRANSITIONS**

A NavStudy Featuring *The* MESSAGE®

Written and compiled by Tim McLaughlin

NAVPRESS®

BRINGING TRUTH TO LIFE

OUR GUARANTEE TO YOU

We believe so strongly in the message of our books that we are making this quality guarantee to you. If for any reason you are disappointed with the content of this book, return the title page to us with your name and address and we will refund to you the list price of the book. To help us serve you better, please briefly describe why you were disappointed. Mail your refund request to: NavPress, P.O. Box 35002, Colorado Springs, CO 80935.

The Navigators is an international Christian organization. Our mission is to advance the gospel of Jesus and His kingdom into the nations through spiritual generations of laborers living and discipling among the lost. We see a vital movement of the gospel, fueled by prevailing prayer, flowing freely through relational networks and out into the nations where workers for the kingdom are next door to everywhere.

NavPress is the publishing ministry of The Navigators. The mission of NavPress is to reach, disciple, and equip people to know Christ and make Him known by publishing life-related materials that are biblically rooted and culturally relevant. Our vision is to stimulate spiritual transformation through every product we publish.

© 2007 by The Navigators

All rights reserved. No part of this publication may be reproduced in any form without written permission from NavPress, P.O. Box 35001, Colorado Springs, CO 80935.
www.navpress.com

NAVPRESS, BRINGING TRUTH TO LIFE, and the NAVPRESS logo are registered trademarks of NavPress. Absence of ® in connection with marks of NavPress or other parties does not indicate an absence of registration of those marks.

ISBN-13: 978-1-60006-164-6
ISBN-10: 1-60006-164-8

Cover design by Chris Gilbert/Studio Gearbox www.studiogearbox.com
Cover image by Andrew Geiger/Getty
Creative Team: John Blase, Cara Iverson, Darla Hightower, Arvid Wallen, Kathy Guist

Written and compiled by Tim McLaughlin

Some of the anecdotal illustrations in this book are true to life and are included with the permission of the persons involved. All other illustrations are composites of real situations, and any resemblance to people living or dead is coincidental.

Unless otherwise identified, all Scripture quotations in this publication are taken from *THE MESSAGE* (msg). Copyright © 1993, 1994, 1995, 1996, 2000, 2001, 2002. Used by permission of NavPress Publishing Group.

Printed in the United States of America

1 2 3 4 5 6 / 11 10 09 08 07

FOR A FREE CATALOG OF NAVPRESS BOOKS & BIBLE STUDIES, CALL
1-800-366-7788 (USA) OR 1-800-839-4769 (CANADA).

contents

about the **REAL**LIFE**STUFF**FOR**COUPLES** series	5
introduction	7
how to use this discussion guide	11
small-group study tips	13
Lesson 1: the unexpected transition	15
Lesson 2: the cataclysmic transition	33
Lesson 3: the masked transition	55
Lesson 4: the partner's transition	71
Lesson 5: the predictable transition	89
Lesson 6: the cultural transition	107
Lesson 7: the final transition	125
Lesson 8: hope for your marriage in transition	143
notes	157

about the REAL LIFE STUFF FOR COUPLES series

> Let your love dictate how you deal with me;
>   teach me from your textbook on life.
> I'm your servant—help me understand what that means,
>   the inner meaning of your instructions. . . .
> Break open your words, let the light shine out,
>   let ordinary people see the meaning.
>
> PSALM 119:124-125,130

We're all yearning for understanding, truth, wisdom, hope. Whether we quietly simmer in uncertainty or boil over into blatant unbelief, we long for a better life, a more meaningful existence, a more fulfilling marriage. We want our marriages to matter—to ourselves, most of all, and then to our children and the rest of our families and friends. But real-life stuff—the urgency of daily life with all its responsibilities, major and minor catastrophes, conversations, dreams, and all—tends to fog up the image of the marriage we crave. And so we go on with the way things are.

We can pretend that there's really no problem, that everything is actually fine, thank you. We can intensify the same old way we've been living, hoping that more is better. We can flee—emotionally, spiritually, literally.

Whether or not we face it head-on, real life matters. In that fog there are things about ourselves, our spouses, and our marriages that cause distress, discomfort, and dis-ease.

The Real Life Stuff for Couples series is a safe place for exploring the truth about that fog. It's not your typical Bible study—no fill-in-the-blank questions, no one telling you what things mean or what to do. In fact, you'll probably finish a Real Life Stuff study with more questions than you started with. But through personal reflection and lively conversation in your small group (you know this is the best part of a Bible study anyway), these books will take you where you need to go—and in the process bring greater hope and meaning to your life.

Each Real Life Stuff for Couples book gives you the space to ask the hard questions about marriage—yours and others'. A space to find comfort in the chaos. A space to enlarge your understanding of your marriage, your God, and where those two intersect.

And—with the guidance of the Holy Spirit—a space to discover real-life hope for your marriage that brings meaning to the everyday challenge of crafting a life together.

introduction

He was seventeen, it was June, and Donnie was somewhere between wistfulness of departing a familiar high school and nervous excitement of starting college on the other side of the country. It was a passage, a time channel. Even from his perspective of two decades older, Donnie vividly remembers the sense of being in transition.

That summer found him in a more literal passage, too: the desert canyons of Central Oregon's John Day River. During a week of canoeing with his high school buddies, there were placid lengths of river when they'd rest their paddles across the gunwales, lean back, float with the lazy current, bask in the high-desert sun, and exchange stories of girlfriends left behind, summer jobs when they got off the river and back home, and college beyond even that.

Connecting those serene stretches of river, however, were sleek liquid chutes dropping four and five feet between golf-cart-sized boulders into roaring whitewater. There were roiling eddies, standing waves of frothing water turned chocolate by that week's afternoon thunderstorms and midnight cloudbursts. Donnie and his buds would shoot these rapids one canoe at a time; and one at a time they'd emerge from the rapids downstream, either in their canoes or in the river itself, swimming to retrieve the stray booties, paddles, and water bottles floating around them. Then the aluminum armada would regroup and launch into the next placid stretch of river.

It is a fair representation of most marriages: long stretches of routine, tedious chores and fixed schedules, punctuated by traumatic or calamitous or even violent events that, ready or not, propel you into a very different inner or outer landscape.

Our pastors and Bible teachers assure us that a relevant Bible holds eternal principles that guarantee safe (if not bloodless) passage through life's flood-stage rapids. And sure enough, the Bible is a roaring success on this point—in fact, most of its marital episodes are nothing *but* transitions of some kind or another. You won't read much about biblical couples doing the dishes, picking up after the dog, signing kids' reports cards. Instead, it's mostly tumultuous transitions, crises involving sex or children or death. (Okay, so there *is* one episode, seasonally prominent, that promises to be maritally mundane: a matter of paying household taxes, and a road trip in order to pay them. Dull, routine, the stuff of uneventful daily life, right? But what could have been a tedious IRS filing is upstaged by the late-term pregnancy of the unmarried girl, by monomaniacal jealousy in high places, and by the divine cause of all this fuss.)

Which leaves us with a Bible that seems to do a more thorough job recording the surprises and catastrophes and crises of transitions than of the other 90 percent of our lives that is mundane and uneventful.

So let us take to heart what the Bible offers in dump-truck quantities: examples of people both in relationship and in transition. Like you and your spouse.

There is another aspect to transitions, however—a darker one, perhaps, certainly less promoted and preached. The absolute, black-and-white truth of the Bible doesn't give us a lot of room for gray, for in-between, for that fuzzy place that's kind of both as well as neither. Yet this is the very terrain of transitions—neither one nor the other, but a typically temporary in-betweenness that, in addition to the inherent stress of your circumstances, often creates a Christian a doctrinal discomfort, a theological anxiety:

- Why is this happening to me, after I followed all the biblical principles in good faith?
- After a decade of regular quiet times with the Lord, how did I end up in this maelstrom?

- This hell I'm in took me by complete surprise. What happened to the promises of God to protect me?

Our church leaders, our friends, our confidants have answers, of course, and some version of their answers is likely correct. God is the blessed controller of all things . . . God never promised his people a life of painlessness . . . Trials (transitions?) are God's way of growing us up and creating maturity in us.

Yet when you're the one up to your ears with a spouse who is reinventing herself, when it's your marriage that is broadsided by an unexpected rush of change, when you finally hit a passage that you've seen coming for a while, when you and your spouse are separated, whether by divorce or by death—during such transitions, you are acutely aware of being *between*, of existing in the gray zone if only for a season, and the black-and-white certainties just don't fit the way they did in calmer waters.

Anticipating such passages—or in the middle of them now—you can still keep faith in God, you can keep supportive friends around you, you can remember that people just like you have survived tumultuous transitions. May this discussion guide trigger conversations among you and other couples, or simply between you and your spouse—conversations that let you prepare as much as possible for those white-water rapids in your life and help you emerge from them stronger, wiser, more faithful, and maybe a little easier to live with.

how to use this discussion guide

This discussion guide is meant to be completed by you and your spouse—*and* in a small group of married couples. So before you dive into this book, put together a discussion group. Maybe the two of you already belong to a couples' group. That works just fine. Or maybe you know three or four couples who could do coffee once a week. That works too. Ask around. You'll be surprised how many of your coworkers, teammates, or neighbors would be interested in a small-group study, especially a study like this that doesn't require vast biblical knowledge. A group of three or four couples is optimal—any bigger and one or more members will likely be shut out of discussions. Or your small group can be only you two and another couple. Choose a couple who are not afraid to talk with you honestly and authentically about themselves. Make sure all participants have their own copies of this book.

1. *Read* the Bible passages and other readings in each lesson as a couple or on your own. Let it all soak in. Then use the white space provided to "think out loud on paper." Note content in the readings that troubles you, inspires you, confuses you, or challenges you. Be honest. Be bold. Don't shy away from the hard things. If you don't understand the passage, say so to your spouse, to your group. If you don't agree, say that, too. You may choose to cover a lesson in one thirty- to forty-five-minute focused session. Or perhaps you'll spend twenty minutes a

day on the readings.

2. *Think* about what you read. Think about what you wrote. Always ask, "What does this mean?" and "Why does this matter?" about the readings. Compare different Bible translations. Respond to the questions we've provided. You may have a lot to say on one topic, little on another. Allow the experience of others to broaden your experience. You'll be stretched here—called upon to evaluate what you've discovered and asked to make practical sense of it. In a group, that stretching can often be painful and sometimes embarrassing. But your willingness to be transparent—your openness to the possibility of personal growth—will reap great rewards.

3. *Pray* as you go through the entire session: before you read a word, in the middle of your thinking process, when you get stuck on a concept or passage, and as you approach the time when you'll explore these passages and thoughts together in a small group. Pray with your spouse, pray by yourself. Pray for inspiration, pray in frustration. Speak your prayers, write your prayers in this book, or let your silence be a prayer.

4. *Live.* (That's "live" as in rhymes with "give" as in "Give me something that will benefit my marriage.") Before you and your spouse meet with your small group, complete as much of this section as you can (particularly the "What I Want to Discuss" section). Then, in your small group, ask the hard questions about what the lesson means to you. (You know, the questions everyone is thinking, but no one is voicing.) Talk with your spouse about relevant, reachable goals. Record your real-world plan in this book. Commit to following through on these plans, and prepare to be held accountable.

5. *Follow up.* Don't let the life application drift away without action. Be accountable to the other couples in your group, and refer to previous "Live" sections often. Take time at the beginning of each new study to review. See how you're doing.

6. *Repeat* as necessary.

small-group study tips

After going through each week's study with your spouse, it's time to sit down with the other couples in your group and go deeper. Here are a few thoughts on how to make the most of your small-group discussion time.

Set ground rules. You don't need many. Here are two:

First, you'll want couples in your group to commit to the entire eight-week study. A binding legal document with notarized signatures and commitments written in blood probably isn't necessary. Just remember this: Significant personal growth happens when group members spend enough time together to really get to know each other. Hit-and-miss attendance rarely allows this to occur.

Second, agree together that everyone's story is important. Time is a valuable commodity, so if you have an hour to spend together, do your best to give each person ample time to express concerns, pass along insights, and generally feel like a participating member of the group. Small-group discussions are not monologues. However, a one-person-dominated discussion isn't always a bad thing. Not only is your role in a small group to explore and expand your own understanding, it's also to support one another. If someone truly needs more of the floor, give it to her. There will be times when the needs of the one outweigh the needs of the many. Use good judgment and allow a person extra time when needed. Your time may be next week.

Meet regularly. Choose a time and place, and stick to it. No one likes a rushed supper and a drop-and-run at the sitter only to arrive at the study and be told, "Oh, didn't you get the message? We canceled tonight's meeting because Julie's out of town." Consistency removes stress that could otherwise frustrate discussion and subsequent personal growth. Come on, it's only eight weeks. You can do this.

Talk openly. If you enter this study with shields up, you're probably not alone. And you're not a "bad person" for hesitating to unpack your life in front of friends or strangers. Maybe you're skeptical about the value of revealing the deepest parts of who you are to others. Maybe you're just not ready to say that much about *that* aspect of your marriage. Really, you don't have to go to a place where you're uncomfortable. If you want to sit and listen, offer a few thoughts, or merely hint at dilemmas in your marriage, go ahead. But don't neglect what brings you to this group of couples — that longing for a better, more satisfying, less tension-filled marriage. Dip your feet in the water of brutally honest conversation, and you may choose to dive in. There is healing here.

Stay on task. Refrain from sharing information that falls into the "too much information" category. Don't spill unnecessary stuff, such as your wife's penchant for midnight belly dancing or your husband's obsession with Sandra Bullock.

If structure isn't your group's strength, try a few minutes of general comments about the study, and then take each "Live" question one at a time and give everyone in the group a chance to respond. That should quickly get you into the meat of matters.

Hold each other accountable. That "Live" section isn't just busywork. If you're ready for positive change in your marriage, take this section seriously. Not only should you be thorough as you summarize your discoveries, practical as you compose your goals, and realistic as you determine the plan for accountability, you must also hold the other couples in the group accountable for doing these things. Be lovingly, brutally honest as you examine each other's "Live" section. Don't hold back — this is where the rubber meets the road. A lack of openness here may send other couples in your group skidding off that road.

lesson 1

the unexpected transition

"What th—?!"—transitions that broadside you with no warning.

the beginning place

The 1968 release of her synthesized *Switched-On Bach* was the perfect example of what, years later, the Moog-influenced composer Wendy Carlos would write on her website: "A nice blend of prediction and surprise seem to be at the heart of the best art."[1]

Carlos may be on to something. For if our experience is any clue, and if God is in the business of (among other enterprises) creating art on the canvas of the universe, then The Predictable and The Surprising certainly describe how most of us perceive our world. Between seasons of regularity, up pops something unexpected. And if you're sharing your life with a wife or husband, what pops up out of the blue is bound to affect not only the two of you but also that mystical third entity alongside the couple: the marriage itself.

Take the surprise that met Della and Matt when they moved to rural America—specifically, five miles outside a small, economically depressed logging town. Raised relentlessly Baptist, they decided one Sunday morning shortly after their move to try out a little country church just down the highway. They parked in the gravel driveway, entered the lobby, and were greeted warmly as visitors. They found aisle seats in the sanctuary and skimmed the bulletin, waiting for the service to begin. All was well—that is, all was predictable and comfortable—until the piano and accordion and guitars kicked in and the congregation around them lifted their faces and arms to the roof, swayed, and sang "I see the Lord" like—well, like they really saw him.

Mind you, this was at a time when worship music wasn't yet a charted genre, when Maranatha! had just released its *Praise 3* (on modern cassettes, even, not eight-tracks), when the Jesus movement converts had only recently gotten married, had children, cut their hair (well, some of them), and put Old Testament psalms and New Testament promises to soft rock. Nor had the practice become common yet of replacing song leaders with worship leaders.

So this was new and different stuff for the couple. Yet Della took to it like a duck to water, for despite the cerebral Christianity she had been raised in, she had always, secretly yearned for more integral spirituality: an expression of her faith that spoke to her feelings and body as well as to her mind.

Matt, on the other hand, was ever the skeptic. After all, these were the people, theirs was the theology, that Matt had warned his students against. The only problem was that this praise music—that, and the love, generosity, and humility of the church's people—touched him in deep places where he had never been touched. Matt couldn't logically reconcile it all in his head. Unlike his wife, it took him years to stop trying to.

It was an unexpected, uncomfortable marital transition for a while due to Della's and Matt's very different spiritual trajectories—Della soaking up what she had always longed for, and Matt resisting, condescending, yet in his own way receiving the unconditional acceptance and friendship those people offered him.

So what transitions in your marriage were unexpected? What suddenly appeared with no warning, requiring a transition to get through or to get used to? What most recently has broadsided you and, in the process, affected your marriage? Are you or your spouse most affected? Which of you is the first to cope calmly with such a surprise, and which of you takes a lot of time to work your way to the end of the transition and back to a kind of normalcy? Use the space below to summarize your beginning place for this lesson. We'll start here and then go deeper.

shooting the rapids in a wooden canoe

read   oops

Luke 1:26-35; Matthew 1:18-25

In the sixth month of Elizabeth's pregnancy, God sent the angel Gabriel to the Galilean village of Nazareth to a virgin engaged to be married to a man descended from David. His name was Joseph, and the virgin's name, Mary. Upon entering, Gabriel greeted her:

> Good morning!
> You're beautiful with God's beauty,
> Beautiful inside and out!
> God be with you.

She was thoroughly shaken, wondering what was behind a greeting like that. But the angel assured her, "Mary, you have nothing to fear. God has a surprise for you: You will become pregnant and give birth to a son and call his name Jesus.

> He will be great,
>   be called 'Son of the Highest.'
> The Lord God will give him
>   the throne of his father David;
> He will rule Jacob's house forever—
>   no end, ever, to his kingdom."

Mary said to the angel, "But how? I've never slept with a man." The angel answered,

> The Holy Spirit will come upon you,
>   the power of the Highest hover over you;
> Therefore, the child you bring to birth
>   will be called Holy, Son of God." . . .

Joseph discovered she was pregnant. (It was by the Holy Spirit, but he didn't know that.) Joseph, chagrined but noble, determined to take care of things quietly so Mary would not be disgraced.

While he was trying to figure a way out, he had a dream. God's angel spoke in the dream: "Joseph, son of David, don't hesitate to get married. Mary's pregnancy is Spirit-conceived. God's Holy Spirit has made her pregnant. She will bring a son to birth, and when she does, you, Joseph, will name him Jesus—'God saves'—because he will save his people from their sins." This would bring the prophet's embryonic sermon to full term:

> Watch for this—a virgin will get pregnant and bear a son;
> They will name him Immanuel (Hebrew for "God is with us").

Then Joseph woke up. He did exactly what God's angel commanded in the dream: He married Mary. But he did not consummate the marriage until she had the baby. He named the baby Jesus.

think

- Whom do you feel was more surprised by the pregnancy, Mary or Joseph? Why?
- Is there anything that makes you believe that the couple explained the pregnancy to others, or do you think they kept the details to themselves? What would have been the fallout from either course they chose?
- What guidance or advice might there be in this biblical episode for today's women and men surprised by a pregnancy?

20 shooting the rapids in a wooden canoe

think (continued)

pray

read   two true loves?

From *Marriage in Motion: The Natural Ebb and Flow of Lasting Relationships*, by Richard Schwartz and Jacqueline Olds[2]

> The important news is that a large portion of affairs start in marriages in which both partners report that they are quite contented. Once someone begins moving closer to another person outside the marriage and is headed toward a sexual relationship, it is difficult to halt the momentum of infatuation and excitement. To ease the conscience, the errant spouse must start to believe that there were already major defects in the marriage or else the affair would never have happened. Our culture's emphasis on "one true love" doesn't help matters any. The implication of this romantic fallacy is that one could never possibly be attracted to a "second true love," certainly not to the point of acting on it, while in a happy marriage. The reality is quite different from the myth. It is quite possible for someone to love or at least care immensely and romantically about two people at the same time. Each mother awaiting the birth of a second child cannot imagine loving the second as much as her first. Yet she is regularly and happily surprised to discover that she comes to love the second equally. We are all very capable of loving more than one person romantically if we let ourselves. Yet we risk losing much that we cherish when we do. The middle years of marriage may be especially risky in this regard. The marriage is anything but new and we tend to take for granted a relationship that has lasted so long.

think

- How do our cultural myths contribute to marital crises?
- How convincing is the writer's claim that "we are all very capable of loving more than one person romantically if we let ourselves"? What makes you agree or disagree with it?

- If you are contented and relatively happy in your own marriage, have you nonetheless ever been blindsided by strong feelings for someone else? How did you deal with those feelings?

pray

read options are nice, but . . .

From *Married: A Fine Predicament*, by Anne Roiphe[3]

There have been opportunities. I am at lunch with a man who has invited me out to discuss a book project he would like to work on with me. Before the coffee arrives he tells me he wants one more adventure in his life before age binds him to his home. I think he wants to climb a mountain or fly an airplane. It seems he wants to have an affair with me. He is appealing. He smiles at me. "What could be wrong?" he says. "It will be our secret." He offers a little excitement that won't hurt anybody. He takes my hand. I am pleased. When you are a married woman this does not happen very often. My feathers must still be shining. Why not? No one would have to know. I could play. I don't believe that sexual pleasure beyond the marital license is a serious sin. I don't believe in my immortal soul. My mortal soul gives me trouble enough. But then I think of something far worse than sin. I could hurt my husband whom I would never hurt, not for a second, and I would hurt him if for even one afternoon I went with this man and let him touch my body that knows so well my husband's body. I would defile the thing we do with each other in the bed when the children are sleeping. I am not sorry the man has asked me. A woman likes to know that her options are still there. But I am certain I will not accept. I am not afraid my husband will find out. I am afraid that my knowing will slide into my life with him, will destroy some absolute closeness we have achieved, will harm us both in some unknown way. I wonder if I am just conventional, afraid of life, too cautious for a swim in the wide sea. That is possible. But I have known what it is like to be alone in the world and I have known that I could not harm my love or even bring it into dangerous waters. Maybe this is fear. Maybe this is what we mean by love. I would not break his trust in me. After all my trust in him is the cornerstone of my life and all would tumble down without it. I drink my coffee and go home.

Monogamy has its price. But it has its rewards too. Would I be a more interesting person, a better lover to my spouse, a wiser woman had I met this one or that one in this place or that? I will never know. What I do know is that, reasonable or not, to be with another man in the ways I am with my husband is unthinkable, would violate the web of life we have spun together, would jar and tear at the very roots of our trust.

think

- When is the last time someone reminded you that "your feathers must still be shining"? How was the reminder communicated?
- How do you feel about the writer's stated motives for remaining faithful to her husband?
- Why do *you* remain faithful?

pray

lesson ONE: the unexpected transition   25

read   the dark side of parenting

From *The Poisonwood Bible*, by Barbara Kingsolver[4]

> Three babies were too much, and I sensed it deep in my body. When the third one was born she could not turn her head to the side or even properly suckle. That was Adah. I'd cried for days when I learned I was carrying twins, and now I lay awake nights wondering whether my despair had poisoned her. . . . The doctors gave her little hope, though one of the nurses was kind. She told me formula was the very best thing, a modern miracle, but we couldn't afford it for two. So I ended up suckling greedy Leah at my breast and giving Adah the expensive bottles, both at the same time; with twins you learn how to do everything backhanded.
>
> Not only twins, mind you, but also a tow-headed toddler, whose skin seemed too thin, for she wailed at the slightest discomfort. Rachel screamed every single time she wet her diaper, and set the other two off like alarm bells. She also screamed excessively over teething. Adah howled from frustration, and Leah cried over nightmares. For six years, from age nineteen until I turned twenty-five, I did not sleep uninterrupted through a single night. There it is. And you wonder why I didn't rise up and revolt against Nathan? I felt lucky to get my shoes on the right feet, that's why. I moved forward only, thinking each morning anew that we were leaving the worst behind.

think

- Have you been in these shoes? If so, how vivid are the memories?
- If you haven't experienced this, what do narratives like this do for any desire you have to be a parent?
- Why do you feel that the first two years of draining, energy-sapping parenting still come as a surprise to most couples? Wouldn't you think that experience this universal could be passed on to younger generations? What gives?

- If you've been through such years, how did you make it? What one or two factors especially got you through it?

pray

lesson ONE: the unexpected transition

read when the wife loses her job

From *The Feminine Journey: Understanding the Biblical Stages of a Woman's Life*, by Cynthia and Robert Hicks[5]

> Whitney has been a working woman from the time she graduated from college. . . . She was putting in ten- to twelve-hour days, six days a week. She enjoyed being a workaholic. Therefore, when Whitney lost her job, she was devastated. . . . "I felt betrayed. One day you're a part of this happy family and the next day you're told you are no longer a part of the family." Whitney assumed if she worked hard and was productive she would be rewarded. According to her way of thinking, "People don't lose their job unless they screw up." Suddenly, her contributions and hard work seemed worthless and meaningless. For the first time, feelings of low self-esteem and negative self-talk hammered away in her mind. . . .
>
> When Whitney went home to share the news with her parents, their reaction was another nail in the coffin. Rather than finding comfort and understanding, she found blame. Her mother's initial response was, "What did you do wrong?" Her mother had never worked outside the home and had no appreciation for what this loss represented to Whitney. Her father had worked for the same company for thirty-five years and had no comprehension of the pain of being fired. They assumed it was her fault that she lost her job. . . .
>
> As she began the painful and tedious process of a job search, Whitney discovered both family and friends to be of little comfort. She commented, "They just don't know how to act around an unemployed person."

think

- What experience do you have being female and being let go from your job—even, perhaps, a volunteer job that you were deeply involved in?

- If you've been in such circumstances, how unexpected was it?
- What in the writer's experience do you most identify with? Least?
- What experience do you have being the *husband* to such a woman?

pray

lesson ONE: the unexpected transition

read how'd I get like this anyway, and how do I change?

From *TrueFaced: Trust God and Others with Who You Really Are*, by Bill Thrall, Bruce McNicol, and John Lynch[6]

Most of us will admit, "I know I wear masks. Sometimes I feel like I'm working off a prepared script. I'll say the most trite-sounding things in order to cover my real feelings. I don't really like this about me, but I have no idea how to take my masks off. If I did, I don't think I would have gotten into this mess."

But if asked where all this junk comes from, most of us couldn't answer. *Most of us are in the dark about how we got like this.* We blame our actions on circumstances of the pressure we're under. "I must be going through menopause or a mid-life crisis," we say. And that makes sense . . . until we are reminded that we aren't yet forty!

One of the really good gifts we could receive would be the ability to see where we are and how we got there. We need to see ourselves in our story, to see what causes and nurtures the responses that trip us up. We must see that our controlling behavior isn't a response to something happening in the present. It was triggered by some sin in the past that never got resolved. If we can begin to understand the phases of unresolved sin and discover what is happening to us, we may no longer react to life like lemmings heading for a cliff.

think

- Describe a time when you reacted to something your spouse said and had no idea where that reaction came from?
- To what degree do you feel in the dark about the source of your responses and reactions to specific moments in your marriage? What triggers those responses—your spouse's words, tone of voice, body language?

- If you have done any counseling or inner work that revealed the causes of your reactions, did the knowledge help? Talk about this.
- If and when you began to investigate the source of your strong reactions to your spouse—whether through therapy or honest conversations with a good friend—did you resist what began to emerge, or did you embrace it?

pray

LIVE

what i want to discuss

What have you discovered this week that you definitely want to discuss with your small group? Write that here. Then begin your small-group discussion with these thoughts.

so what?

Use the following space to summarize what you've discovered during this chapter about finding your way through unexpected transitions—shifts in the life of your marriage that broadside you from out of nowhere. Review your Beginning Place if you need to remember where you began. How does God's truth impact the next step in your journey?

then what?

What is one practical thing you can do to apply what you've discovered? Describe how you will put this into practice. What steps will you take? Remember to think realistically; an admirable but unreachable goal is as good as no goal. Discuss your goal with your small group to further define it.

how?

Identify how you will be held accountable to the goal you described. Who will be on your support team? What are their responsibilities? How will you measure the success of your plan? Write the details here.

lesson 2

the cataclysmic transition

"Oh my God, I'm gonna die"—crises that press your marriage to the breaking point.

the beginning place

> Like a plant that starts up in showers and sunshine and does not know which has best helped it to grow, I find it difficult to say whether the hard things or the pleasant things did me the most good.
>
> —Lucy Larcom[1]

There are rough patches in a marriage, and then there are rough patches. We're not talking an emotional dry spell between you and your spouse (say, a month or two of exhausting eighteen-hour days that drain all your energy and time away from your primary relationships) or a harried season (mother-in-law comes to live with you for a while). These may tax your marriage, but they don't make you feel like dying.

Going through a cataclysmic passage, you're convinced that something is about to break—you, your spirit, your faith, your marriage. The crisis threatens to undo you. Friends can assure you that it's only a transition, that you will emerge from this passage as a survivor, but you know better. You're going to die in a pile, if not today, then tomorrow.

"Any idiot can face a crisis," Anton Chekhov is reported to have said. "It's the day-to-day living that wears you out."[2] Maybe so, but when it's *you* in a maelstrom of a transition, you'd rather punch him than agree with him. In such a suffocating crisis, you long for the day-to-day living and would, without a second thought, exchange your hellish suffering for mere mundane life.

We're warned about such passages. *They are temporary,* we are told. *They will pass. Just hold firm and endure and all will be well—eventually*. And, of course, our encouragers are right; the problem is believing them even as the breath is being squeezed out of you.

And out of your marriage, too. What marital relationship *isn't* affected by a severe financial downturn? By loss of your job followed by loss of your spouse's job followed by loss of house? By a life-threatening or even terminal health crisis in your immediate family? By any one of a number of ways you can cheat on your spouse (not just the unequivocal, monthly, or weekly sex from noon till three but also affairs of the heart—or Internet fantasies, strip-club tease, or wherever away from your spouse you willingly let yourself be drawn)?

One thinks of Job, that ancient, bearded, biblical victim who soldiered through unspeakable misery—including the loss of his children. Those were the children of Job's wife, too, and you can nearly hear the bitter, excruciating pain in her voice when she tells her husband to pack it in, curse God, and be done with it—unload his precious integrity since she for one sees no integrity in heaven.

That old Mesopotamian marriage survived the cataclysm though. Pressed to the breaking point, Job and his wife somehow made it out the other side of inexplicable hardship—and not just made it out but also managed to find the emotional wherewithal to engender a second family of children.

Maybe Job's experience shows the best and worst of what a season or passage of cataclysmic crisis can do to a marriage: not only test it to the nth degree, but maybe strengthen it, too.

lesson TWO: the cataclysmic transition

So what hellish transition are you in the grip of now? If not now, recall one from earlier in your marriage. What was the nature of this crisis? What was its effect on your marriage? How receptive were you to encouragement from people outside your marriage? What good decisions did you make during that transition? What decisions do you regret making during that passage? Use the space below to summarize your beginning place for this lesson. We'll start here and then go deeper.

read   bad times

From *Married: A Fine Predicament*, by Anne Roiphe[3]

>[My husband's] play that opened on Broadway was panned, not a little but a lot, made fun of, ridiculed cruelly. On opening night we read the reviews at a party at a beautiful restaurant with blue lights blinking in the palm fronds. He left the party alone and went drinking for days and days without calling or letting me know that he was alive and well. I went home to our baby. By then I knew we weren't in this together and not forever. I didn't stop loving him then. It took a long time and many aftershocks for that affection to wither and change and eventually die down to indifference or something close to that.
>
>Bad times are good indicators of the state of a marriage. Three months later he left the apartment with a suitcase. We did not part because of the play's failure. We parted because the failure of the play exposed the fact that there was no "we," that I couldn't save him from himself and should stop trying. He left me because I was no longer a talisman of good luck. Our mutual endeavor had crashed. He left me the way one leaves the scene of an accident, quickly.
>
>There are men who are so ashamed of a failure that they can't face their families and they run away. I suspect that during the depression the railroads carried many such men in different directions all away from the persons who loved them. But if a marriage can contain the disappointment of one partner or the other, can struggle through economic reverses, or professional failures, if a man and a woman hold tight to each other when the world seems most rejecting, then marriage serves its purpose. But if bad times sap all the energy, bring out the worst, kill the hope that originally kindled the love, then marriage, always a fragile matter, can be damaged beyond repair. It's all very easy to say the words, "for better or worse," but to mean it is another matter entirely.
>
>We are selfish creatures after all. To stay with a man who has lost his ability to support the family, to respect him and never

resent him, to keep on acting cheerful against the evidence, to fan the flame of erotic love under those circumstances, that requires a heroic effort beyond many mere mortals. These are thoughts I file under the category of money, money matters. Not just money but good fortune matters. What happens to a marriage is not always ours to shape. Fate, luck, history, the outside universe, they get to play with us and our marriages. No avoiding that.

think

- "Bad times are good indicators of the state of a marriage," Roiphe writes. Describe a bad time in your marriage and what it revealed about your marriage.
- Do you think it's possible that a marriage can be damaged beyond repair by a bad stretch—that there is simply no remedying some marriages? Why or why not?
- What might be the thing that could make you *flee* your marriage?
- Now reverse that question: What's the thing that could make you *hold fast* to your spouse and marriage during a bad time?

pray

38 shooting the rapids in a wooden canoe

read when your child dies

2 Samuel 11:2-5,14-15,26-27; 12:13-24

One late afternoon, David got up from taking his nap and was strolling on the roof of the palace. From his vantage point on the roof he saw a woman bathing. The woman was stunningly beautiful. David sent to ask about her, and was told, "Isn't this Bathsheba, daughter of Eliam and wife of Uriah the Hittite?" David sent his agents to get her. After she arrived, he went to bed with her. (This occurred during the time of "purification" following her period.) Then she returned home. Before long she realized she was pregnant.

Later she sent word to David: "I'm pregnant." . . .

In the morning David wrote a letter to Joab and sent it with Uriah. In the letter he wrote, "Put Uriah in the front lines where the fighting is the fiercest. Then pull back and leave him exposed so that he's sure to be killed." . . .

When Uriah's wife heard that her husband was dead, she grieved for her husband. When the time of mourning was over, David sent someone to bring her to his house. She became his wife and bore him a son. . . .

David confessed to [the prophet] Nathan, "I've sinned against God."

Nathan pronounced, "Yes, but that's not the last word. God forgives your sin. You won't die for it. But because of your blasphemous behavior, the son born to you will die."

After Nathan went home, God afflicted the child that Uriah's wife bore to David, and he came down sick. David prayed desperately to God for the little boy. He fasted, wouldn't go out, and slept on the floor. The elders in his family came in and tried to get him off the floor, but he wouldn't budge. Nor could they get him to eat anything. On the seventh day the child died. David's servants were afraid to tell him. They said, "What do we do now? While the child was living he wouldn't listen to a word we said.

Now, with the child dead, if we speak to him there's no telling what he'll do."

David noticed that the servants were whispering behind his back, and realized that the boy must have died.

He asked the servants, "Is the boy dead?"

"Yes," they answered. "He's dead."

David got up from the floor, washed his face and combed his hair, put on a fresh change of clothes, then went into the sanctuary and worshiped. Then he came home and asked for something to eat. They set it before him and he ate.

His servants asked him, "What's going on with you? While the child was alive you fasted and wept and stayed up all night. Now that he's dead, you get up and eat."

"While the child was alive," he said, "I fasted and wept, thinking God might have mercy on me and the child would live. But now that he's dead, why fast? Can I bring him back now? I can go to him, but he can't come to me."

David went and comforted his wife Bathsheba. And when he slept with her, they conceived a son. When he was born they named him Solomon.

From *The Oxford Book of Marriage*, edited by Helge Rubinstein[4]

Part of a letter from Emma Darwin, pregnant with their ninth child, to her husband, Charles, who was taking care of their dying ten-year-old daughter, Annie; 1851.

> My feelings of longing after our lost treasure make me feel painfully indifferent to the other children but I shall get right in my feelings to them before long. You must remember that you are my prime treasure (and always have been) my only hope of consolation is to have you safe home and weep together. I feel so full of fears about you, they are not reasonable fears but my power of hoping seems gone.

Charles's letter announcing the little girl's death followed shortly after:

My dearest Emma,

    I pray God Fanny's note may have prepared you. She went to her final sleep most tranquilly, most sweetly at 12 o'clock today. Our poor dear child had had a very short life but I trust happy and God only knows what miseries might have been in store for her. She expired without a sigh. How desolate it makes one to think of her frank cordial manners. I am so thankful for the daguerreotype, I cannot remember ever seeing the dear child naughty, God bless her. We must be more and more to each other my dear wife—Do what you can to bear up and think how invariably kind and tender you have been to her—I am in bed not very well with my stomach. When I shall return I cannot yet say. My own poor dear, dear wife.

think

- Two couples who experienced losses. What differences did you detect in their circumstances? What were the differences in their reactions to their tragic losses?
- What similarities were there in the circumstances of these two couples' losses? Similarities in their reactions?
- In what ways can you imagine that the death of a child can stress the parents' marriage to the breaking point?
- How near to this kind of tragedy have you been? What was the effect of the child's death on the parents' marriage?

think (continued)

pray

read financial disaster

From *The Essential Rumi*, translated by Coleman Barks with John Moyne[5]

A Man and a Woman Arguing
One night in the desert
a poor Bedouin woman has this to say
to her husband,
"Everyone is happy
and prosperous, except us! We have no bread.
We have no spices. We have no water jug.
We barely have any clothes. No blankets
for the night. We fantasize that the full moon
is a cake. We reach for it! We're an embarrassment
even to the beggars. Everyone avoids us.
Arab men are supposed to be generous warriors,
but look at you, stumbling around! If some guest
were to come to us, we'd steal his rags
when he fell asleep. Who is your guide
that leads you to this! We can't even get
a handful of lentils! Ten years' worth
of nothing, that's what we are!"
She went on and on.
"If God is abundant, we must be following
an imposter. Who's leading us? Some fake,
that always says, *Tomorrow, illumination
will bring you treasure, tomorrow.*
As everyone knows, that never comes.
Though I guess, it happens very rarely, sometimes
that a disciple following an imposter can somehow
surpass the pretender. But still I want to know
what this deprivation says about us."
The husband replied, finally,
"How long will you complain
about money and our prospects for money? The torrent
of our life has mostly gone by. Don't worry about

transient things. Think how the animals live.
The dove on the branch giving thanks.
The glorious singing of the nightingale.
The gnat. The elephant. Every living thing
trusts in God for its nourishment.
These pains that you feel are messengers.
Listen to them. Turn them to sweetness. The night
is almost over. You were young once, and content.
Now you think about money all the time.
You used to be that money. You were a healthy vine.
Now you're a rotten fruit. You ought to be growing
sweeter and sweeter, but you've gone bad.
As my wife, you should be equal to me.
Like a pair of boots, if one is too tight,
the pair is of no use.
Like two folding doors, we can't be mismatched.
A lion does not mate with a wolf."

think

- Are these lines about a nagging wife and her contented husband? Or about a realistic wife and her lazy husband? Talk about this.
- Consider couples you've known that have suffered disastrous financial downturns. How did they cope? Did they?
- Recall the closest you've been to a cataclysmic money crisis? How did you survive (if you survived)? Can you name any strengths that crisis gave your marriage? What about scars?

44 shooting the rapids in a wooden canoe

think (continued)

pray

read bed of roses, bed of nails

From *Brave Enough to Follow: What Jesus Can Do When You Keep Your Eyes on Him*, by Stuart Briscoe[6]

> There was a lot more to being Jesus' disciple than Peter had ever imagined. Many of his previously held and deeply cherished ideas were seriously challenged. But amidst his bewilderment and uncertainty, Peter kept on following. His Master had set out for Jerusalem, where it seemed untold horror possibly awaited, but Peter steadfastly followed. Puzzled and troubled, but loyal and brave. A good man despite his obvious flaws. . . .
>
> Jesus doesn't promise that following him will be an easy road. Like Peter, we are in for some surprises when we commit to Christ. His expectations are rigorous. We meet with disappointments. The rewards don't always seem to compensate for the trouble. But by focusing on the blessings, the love, and the grace that flow from him, we gain the fortitude to keep following.

think

- How does your experience compare with what this writer predicts for you as a Christian?
- Bewilderment, uncertainty, surprises, rigorous expectations, disappointments, uncompensated trouble—in light of this writer's description, how would you recommend a specifically *Christian* marriage to a friend?
- How would you respond to someone saying, "I have no time or patience with a passive-aggressive God who dumps on you, then promises to help you through it"?

46   shooting the rapids in a wooden canoe

think (continued)

pray

read   infidelity and its likelihood

1 Corinthians 5:1-5

I also received a report of scandalous sex within your church family, a kind that wouldn't be tolerated even outside the church: One of your men is sleeping with his stepmother. And you're so above it all that it doesn't even faze you! Shouldn't this break your hearts? Shouldn't it bring you to your knees in tears? Shouldn't this person and his conduct be confronted and dealt with? . . .

   I'm telling you that this is wrong. You must not simply look the other way and hope it goes away on its own. Bring it out in the open and deal with it in the authority of Jesus our Master. Assemble the community. . . . Hold this man's conduct up to public scrutiny. Let him defend it if he can! But if he can't, then out with him! It will be totally devastating to him, of course, and embarrassing to you. But better devastation and embarrassment than damnation. You want him on his feet and forgiven before the Master on the Day of Judgment.

Karen S. Peterson, in *USA Today*, December 21, 1998[7]

> About 24% of men and 14% of women have had sex outside their marriages. . . .
>
>   Still, statistics are "really shaky," says Maggie Scarf, author of *Intimate Partners: Patterns in Love and Marriage.* "And what do they mean?" The polls, she says, lump together "one-night stands and intense, long-term affairs."
>
>   People routinely lie to investigators about infidelity, cautions Peggy Vaughan, author of *The Monogamy Myth*. "You cannot trust anybody on a subject like this." She believes about 60% of men and 40% of women will have an extramarital affair at some time; since these people are not always married to each other, about 80% of marriages are touched.

From *Monogamy*, by Adam Phillips[8]

> Infidelity is such a problem because we take monogamy for granted; we treat it as the norm. Perhaps we should take infidelity for granted, assume it with unharrassed ease. Then we would be able to think about monogamy.

think

- To what degree is it true for you that talking about the potential of infidelity helps prevent it?
- Describe the best-case and worst-case effects on marriages from affairs among people you know.
- What strikes you as more effective: assuming monogamy as the norm and working to preserve it, or assuming infidelity as the norm and working to avoid it? Why?

pray

read   the mother of all marital cataclysms

Genesis 3:6-13,16-24; 4:1-16

When the Woman saw that the tree looked like good eating and realized what she would get out of it—she'd know everything!—she took and ate the fruit and then gave some to her husband, and he ate.

Immediately the two of them did "see what's really going on"—saw themselves naked! They sewed fig leaves together as makeshift clothes for themselves.

When they heard the sound of God strolling in the garden in the evening breeze, the Man and his Wife hid in the trees of the garden, hid from God.

God called to the Man: "Where are you?"

He said, "I heard you in the garden and I was afraid because I was naked. And I hid."

God said, "Who told you you were naked? Did you eat from that tree I told you not to eat from?"

The Man said, "The Woman you gave me as a companion, she gave me fruit from the tree, and, yes, I ate it."

God said to the Woman, "What is this that you've done?"

"The serpent seduced me," she said, "and I ate." . . .

    He told the Woman:
"I'll multiply your pains in childbirth;
    you'll give birth to your babies in pain.
You'll want to please your husband,
    but he'll lord it over you."

    He told the Man:
"Because you listened to your wife
    and ate from the tree
That I commanded you not to eat from,
    'Don't eat from this tree,'

> The very ground is cursed because of you;
>> getting food from the ground
> Will be as painful as having babies is for your wife;
>> you'll be working in pain all your life long.
> The ground will sprout thorns and weeds,
>> you'll get your food the hard way,
> Planting and tilling and harvesting,
>> sweating in the fields from dawn to dusk,
> Until you return to that ground yourself, dead and buried;
>> you started out as dirt, you'll end up dirt."

The Man, known as Adam, named his wife Eve because she was the mother of all the living.

God made leather clothing for Adam and his wife and dressed them.

God said, "The Man has become like one of us, capable of knowing everything, ranging from good to evil. What if he now should reach out and take fruit from the Tree-of-Life and eat, and live forever? Never—this cannot happen!"

So God expelled them from the Garden of Eden and sent them to work the ground, the same dirt out of which they'd been made. He threw them out of the garden and stationed angel-cherubim and a revolving sword of fire east of it, guarding the path to the Tree-of-Life.

Adam slept with Eve his wife. She conceived and had Cain. She said, "I've gotten a man, with God's help!"

Then she had another baby, Abel. Abel was a herdsman and Cain a farmer.

Time passed. Cain brought an offering to God from the produce of his farm. Abel also brought an offering, but from the firstborn animals of his herd, choice cuts of meat. God liked Abel and his offering, but Cain and his offering didn't get his approval. Cain lost his temper and went into a sulk.

God spoke to Cain: "Why this tantrum? Why the sulking? If you do well, won't you be accepted? And if you don't do well, sin is lying in wait for you, ready to pounce; it's out to get you, you've got to master it."

Cain had words with his brother. They were out in the field; Cain came at Abel his brother and killed him.

God said to Cain, "Where is Abel your brother?"

He said, "How should I know? Am I his babysitter?"

God said, "What have you done! The voice of your brother's blood is calling to me from the ground. From now on you'll get nothing but curses from this ground; you'll be driven from this ground that has opened its arms to receive the blood of your murdered brother. You'll farm this ground, but it will no longer give you its best. You'll be a homeless wanderer on Earth."

Cain said to God, "My punishment is too much. I can't take it! You've thrown me off the land and I can never again face you. I'm a homeless wanderer on Earth and whoever finds me will kill me."

God told him, "No. Anyone who kills Cain will pay for it seven times over." God put a mark on Cain to protect him so that no one who met him would kill him.

Cain left the presence of God and lived in No-Man's-Land, east of Eden.

think

- Is it tragic, fitting, unfair, or predictable that humankind's first couple found themselves in such a bloody and determinative mess?
- How would you respond to someone saying, "Our racial mother and father were in such a dire marital catastrophe that they didn't just *think* they were going to die, they actually died"?
- Overlook for a moment, if you can, the eternal nature of Adam and Eve's decision. What was the essence of Adam and Eve's dilemma and decision? Of the cause of conflict between their children? Do these root issues show up in your marriage too?

shooting the rapids in a wooden canoe

think (continued)

pray

LIVE

what i want to discuss

What have you discovered this week that you definitely want to discuss with your small group? Write that here. Then begin your small-group discussion with these thoughts.

so what?

Use the following space to summarize what you've discovered during this chapter about coping in the middle of catastrophic transitions in the life of your marriage. Review your Beginning Place if you need to remember where you began. How does God's truth impact the next step in your journey?

then what?

What is one practical thing you can do to apply what you've discovered? Describe how you will put this into practice. What steps will you take? Remember to think realistically; an admirable but unreachable goal is as good as no goal. Discuss your goal with your small group to further define it.

how?

Identify how you will be held accountable to the goal you described. Who will be on your support team? What are their responsibilities? How will you measure the success of your plan? Write the details here.

the masked transition

"What transition? . . . Oh, yeah, I guess if you look at it that way."—unrecognized, disguised passages in the middle of which you wake up one morning, never having seen exactly how your marriage got there.

the beginning place

Seldom are human decisions or changes made without a process of one kind or another. A cabinet secretary suddenly announces her resignation. The evangelical pastor of a megachurch known for opposing gay marriage stuns his congregation with the announcement that he has had a homosexual affair. An eighteen-year-old tells his mother over dinner that he joined the National Guard that day.

Such announcements only *look* sudden. The forces that put the secretary and the pastor out of leadership and put the new recruit in the armed forces roiled and simmered for some time. Of such gradual transitions, most people see only the conclusion of the transition. "It was so sudden!" they exclaim. Actually, it was not as sudden as it looked—there was a process behind each one, whether a month of personal mulling or an intense day of closed-door committee meetings.

But it *was* masked. There was plenty of backstory; it's just that, most of the time, we don't know it.

In a marriage, all sorts of things can mask a transition. The farmers on their stools at the Copper Kettle, hands wrapped around their coffee mugs—*they* see no transition in their neighbor's bad fortune. "After a dozen years of marriage, one day Cindy wakes up a slut," one says, and they shake their heads in disbelief. On Sunday, Bob and Cindy were happily married, church attendees, parents of a couple teenagers; the next Friday Cindy was publicly taking up with a nineteen-year-old convenience store clerk, and the next week they drove out of town together for good.

Kids are clearly one big mask to any number of fissures and shifts deep inside your marriage. "I felt that Carl always came home from work to the kids, not to me," remembers Margie. "Then he'd fall asleep reading to the kids in bed at night. I mean, who's going to fault him for being anything less than a stellar dad? But at the end of the day, there was none of him left for me."

In the most self-sacrificial kind of job—and especially in Christian ministry—work can become one's lover, gradually replacing the spouse. Even in what looks like—even *feels* like, most of the time—a Christian, healthy, happy, God-honoring marriage.

Parents can camouflage an adult child's transition. You've probably seen the scenario: The expectations and easily bruised sensitivities of a parent keep an adult child's behavior in check. When that parent dies, however, the check disappears, and hitherto latent and masked attitudes in the adult child go public, for better or for worse.

Or this subtle, unconscious transition: A couple with one or two or three young children are desperate for just one evening out, away from children, if only for a couple hours. So they secure the services of a teenage girl in their church's youth group, and for a couple years (until the girl leaves for college) the wife and husband enjoy weekly movies or mall browsing or soup and salad at a downtown café. A decade later they hit a rough patch in their marriage, and for a year or so they really don't like each other very much, sex drops to next to nothing, they each wonder about what life outside this marriage would look like—in fact, the only thing that keeps them together, however tenuously, is friendship, their children, and memories of those date nights together.

So what under-the-radar transitions have you recently become aware of? What about your marriage have you or your spouse only lately become aware of? Is there anything your spouse has been insinuating regularly to you but you don't get, don't see? Any trends in your marriage that don't often reach your consciousness but that are chipping away at your marriage? Use the space below to summarize your beginning place for this lesson. We'll start here and then go deeper.

read   the slow drift

From *Middlemarch*, by George Eliot[1]

> He went out of the house, but as his blood cooled he felt that the chief result of the discussion was a deposit of dread within him at the idea of opening with his wife in future subjects which might again urge him to violent speech. It was as if a fracture in delicate crystal had begun, and he was afraid of any movement that might make it fatal. His marriage would be a mere piece of bitter irony if they could not go on loving each other. He had long ago made up his mind to what he thought was her negative character—her want of sensibility, which showed itself in disregard both of his specific wishes and of his general aims. The first great disappointment had been borne: the tender devotedness and docile adoration of the ideal wife must be renounced, and life must be taken up on a lower stage of expectation, as it is by men who have lost their limbs. But the real wife had not only her claims, she had still a hold on his heart, and it was his intense desire that the hold should remain strong. In marriage, the certainty, "She will never love me much," is easier to bear than the fear, "I shall love her no more." Hence, after that outburst, his inward effort was entirely to excuse her, and to blame the hard circumstances which were partly his fault. He tried that evening, by petting her, to heal the wound he had made in the morning, and it was not in Rosamond's nature to be repellent or sulky; indeed, she welcomed the signs that her husband loved her and was under control. But this was something quite distinct from loving *him*.

think

- Did you (or do you) notice in your parents' marriage a lowering of expectations? What did it look like?
- Do you feel that "a lower stage of expectation" regarding your marriage is inevitable or avoidable? If inevitable, is that a bad

thing? Is lowering your expectations of a marriage resigning yourself to second best, or is it a mark of maturity and realism?
- Earlier in your marriage, what signs did you and your spouse exchange that you both took to mean love but that now you see signified something else entirely? If not love, what exactly *did* those signs and gestures indicate?

pray

read   what's an erotic tickle worth to you?

From Cristina Nehring's book review of *Mating in Captivity: Reconciling the Erotic and the Domestic*, by Esther Perel[2]

> Perel practices couples therapy in New York, and her book's organizing principle emerges in a series of clinical vignettes. A typical one might go like this: One spunky young couple has it all. They adore each other. They have wonderful times, wonderful families, spectacular careers. But they are "*in despair over what's happening to them.*" "We are terrified," they confess. Why? Because their sex together is good, dear reader, but it is not *great*.
>
> Incalculable woe. Part of us wonders if Perel might best advise such couples to *get a life*—i.e., *care about something more important*. Go help the homeless or the victims of war, and let your libido rebound on its own time. But the advice Perel proffers her "distressed" clients is not to help others; it is to destroy themselves. Do you, she asks them, express physical affection? "Do you cuddle? . . . Do you touch each other?" Yes, they say, in unison. Well, announces the doctor, "*it's got to stop.*" She gives them an assignment: Stop being nice to each other. Stop kissing. Stop hugging. It is sapping your sexual energy. Treat each other like trash, and you might notice a discreet rise in sexual tension. Or just tension in general, one is tempted to add: "About a month into it," he says, "I wanted nothing more to do with her." Dr. Perel considers this plan a success. "I knew I was onto something."
>
> It's easy to make fun of this sort of thing—and it's important to do so. For the suggestions Perel offers are repellent, as are the assumptions that underlie them: that sex is our only raison d'être, and that it's great to forfeit emotional contact for an extra erotic tickle. That said, Perel *is* onto something. The ironies of intimacy she discusses in her book are real. The paradoxes to which she points—that the cozy closeness of marriage does not often promote unruly desire; that children, the fruit of eros, are sometimes simultaneously its end; and that knowing everything about a person domestically or psychologically does not always make one

crave that person biblically—are real. And they are worth talking about.

think

- How has sex changed for you during the course of your marriage?
- Why do you think the author feels that cozy domesticity dampens rather than inflames sexual appetites in a marriage?
- Is your tendency to follow this trend into your marriage or battle it (in some way, if not Perel's way)?

pray

read   cold war

From *Wobegon Boy*, by Garrison Keillor[3]

She said, "You know what would be the nicest thing? If your parents could come for Thanksgiving." I said I'd get on the phone and invite them. "No, really," she said. "And if they can't come out here, maybe we should go there."

"I'm not sure that's a good idea," I said. "My father collects stuff like you wouldn't believe. Ever since he retired, he's been going to auctions full-time, and the house is a warehouse. It's depressing. . . . We could go up to Amherst and spend Thanksgiving with *your* parents. Wouldn't that be more fun?"

She let that hang in the air for a few miles. "Spending Thanksgiving with my parents would be like being in a bad play and not knowing your lines. They . . . are both active in saving the world and everything is quite civil between them except that they truly despise each other. My mother is an accomplished sufferer. She got the idea as a child that misery was a sign of intelligence. She had some kind of nervous breakdown when she was seventeen, and she has maintained it for forty years. My father is your classic passive-aggressive. They're two spiders weaving a gummy web around each other, constantly hunting each other, always escaping, and no, thank you very much."

think

- Describe a marriage you know about which you've thought, *How did they* get *that way?*
- Why do you think people who despise each other remain married?
- Do you feel there's a way to detect this kind of toxicity in a person *before* you marry them, and thereby avoid such a marriage? Or is it the combination of otherwise healthy personalities that dooms some marriages to this sort of cold war?

lesson THREE: the masked transition 63

think (continued)

pray

read mystical union, or messy union?

From "Pillow Talk: A Conversation with Stephen and Ondrea Levine About Lust, the Meaning of Marriage, and True Intimacy," by Nina Utne[4]

> *Someone wrote that 35 percent of his relationship comes from the fact that he brings his wife a cup of coffee in bed every morning.*

Stephen Levine: What a weak relationship! Boy, that's a miserable relationship. This guy better get himself another hobby!
Ondrea Levine: I was just thinking how very thoughtful that is. Serving each other is exceptionally important.
Stephen: Growth. Growth is also important.
Ondrea: Yes, various levels of growth, but certainly heart expansion. Everybody would define growth so differently, but love has to grow, your heart has to open more, you have to get clearer about your intentions, clearer about what you really want out of this very short life.

And it's so individual; it depends so much on life experience. Love and simple human kindness are of huge value to me, and I find that I'm drawn to people who are thoughtful and kind. I used to be drawn to people who were only wise.

> *It seems like the bottom line is the level of consciousness and open-heartedness that we bring to a long-term relationship.*

Stephen: In a relationship, we're working on a mystical union. That's a term that came from the Christian tradition, but it's part of almost all devotional traditions. And it means uniting at a level way beyond our separation. After 26 years, the line between Ondrea and the Beloved is very, very blurred. In that context, you may ask what happens when two people's goals change. Well, if they're working on becoming whole human beings, they'll change in a whole way, whether it means being together or separate.

Growth and service and practice are important. But what happens if you have those intentions but there are kids and hectic lives and petty annoyances and betrayals? How does mystical union accommodate that?

Stephen: But that's what everybody has to work with. I mean, if you can't get through that stuff, there is no mystical union. If only mystical union were so easy—if people could just lean into each other's soul space, as it were. In fact, people think they're doing that, and it's actually lust, generally. We say that love is as close as you get to God without really trying. When people live together, maybe they do feel each other's souls, maybe they do feel the Beloved, maybe they both enter the Beloved. But mind arises, preference arises, attitude arises, inclination arises.

Ondrea: We raised three kids, and we certainly had our share of times when our hearts were closed to each other and we felt separate, but our commitment was to work on that and to work with it by trying to stay open, trying to understand the other person's conditioning, because our conditionings were so different.

think

- "I'm drawn to people who are thoughtful and kind," said Ondrea. "I used to be drawn to people who were only wise." What kind of person are you now drawn to that you weren't earlier in your life? How, if at all, has your marriage affected that change?
- When did you first become conscious that your sacred, all-consuming love affair with your new wife or husband was being diluted by your own mind, preferences, attitudes, inclinations? How did this transition affect your marriage?
- If you've had children, how (if at all) did they mask little or big trends in your marriage? When did you finally become aware of those trends?

think (continued)

pray

read   a sword and a healing

From *A Grief Observed*, by C. S. Lewis[5]

> There is, hidden or flaunted, a sword between the sexes till an entire marriage reconciles them. It is arrogance in us to call frankness, fairness, and chivalry "masculine" when we see them in a woman; it is arrogance in them, to describe a man's sensitiveness or tact or tenderness as "feminine." But also what poor, warped fragments of humanity most mere men and mere women must be to make the implications of that arrogance plausible. Marriage heals this. Jointly the two become fully human. "In the image of God created He *them*." Thus, by a paradox, this carnival of sexuality leads us out beyond our sexes.

think

- Lewis describes here a subtle transition within marriage—a passage that couples are seldom conscious of but that many (though hardly all) experience. How did you perceive that "sword between the sexes" before, or early in, your marriage?
- In what ways is the wife in your marriage "masculine"? How is the husband "feminine"?
- In what ways has your marriage healed each of you in this regard? Take some time here; these are deep truths in your relationship.

pray

read don't do it, honey

Matthew 27:15-19,24-26

It was an old custom during the Feast for the governor to pardon a single prisoner named by the crowd. At the time, they had the infamous Jesus Barabbas in prison. With the crowd before him, Pilate said, "Which prisoner do you want me to pardon: Jesus Barabbas, or Jesus the so-called Christ?" He knew it was through sheer spite that they had turned Jesus over to him.

While court was still in session, Pilate's wife sent him a message: "Don't get mixed up in judging this noble man. I've just been through a long and troubled night because of a dream about him." . . .

When Pilate saw that he was getting nowhere and that a riot was imminent, he took a basin of water and washed his hands in full sight of the crowd, saying, "I'm washing my hands of responsibility for this man's death. From now on, it's in your hands. You're judge and jury."

The crowd answered, "We'll take the blame, we and our children after us."

Then he pardoned Barabbas. But he had Jesus whipped, and then handed over for crucifixion.

think

- Judging from the husband's and wife's words, what gradual shifts in their lives or their marriage might have unwittingly brought them to this point?
- Why do you feel that Pilate discarded his wife's message? Or *did* he?
- What kind of situation in the life of your marriage do you fear awakening to one day and realizing that you really have no choice anymore in how that situation unfolds?

think (continued)

pray

LIVE

what i want to discuss

What have you discovered this week that you definitely want to discuss with your small group? Write that here. Then begin your small-group discussion with these thoughts.

so what?

Use the following space to summarize what you've discovered during this chapter about transitions so subtle in your marriage that you've woken up to them only after you've been in them a while, or even after you've passed through them. Review your Beginning Place if you need to remember where you began. How does God's truth impact the next step in your journey?

then what?

What is one practical thing you can do to apply what you've discovered? Describe how you will put this into practice. What steps will you take? Remember to think realistically; an admirable but unreachable goal is as good as no goal. Discuss your goal with your small group to further define it.

how?

Identify how you will be held accountable to the goal you described. Who will be on your support team? What are their responsibilities? How will you measure the success of your plan? Write the details here.

lesson 4

the partner's transition

Like it or not, your marriage is changing—and not due to any passage you're going through: You're living with a spouse who is in a transition that you're not part of.

the beginning place

A spouse can feel so helpless sometimes. Even if you're not a fixer by nature, when you see someone as close to you as your wife or husband, you want to at least lessen the pain, the mental agony, the emotional hurt, or just the draining, straining arduousness of whatever passage your lover is working through.

When her young son drowned at summer camp, Trina grieved hard and clean; she somehow retained her trust in God during that first hellishly difficult year. Her husband, on the other hand, spent years in denial, silence, back-burner depression, and a smoldering, confused anger at God.

Before the drowning, they were both steady, stable, devout, and ministering Christians; they are that again. But Phil's muddy and protracted grief had a curious, subtle selfishness to it. If your theology had been blasted by such a tragedy, you too would probably spend a few years in the bomb crater, sifting through the shards of your beliefs, fingering the charred remnants of convictions and dogmas—and in the process, not paying a lot of attention to anyone else, Trina or otherwise.

As necessary as this all may have been for him to get on his emotional and spiritual feet again, Phil wasn't easy to live with for a long while. Trina tried to comfort, tried to talk to him, tried to show her husband the same path out of hopelessness that she had taken. But it wasn't his path, and if she ended up tiptoeing around him for many, many months, it wasn't for lack of trying to connect. Phil had to do what he needed to do, in his way, by his timetable. And meanwhile, Trina waited (and worked, and started on her master's degree).

With Clarissa it was less a timetable than a fuse. When her firstborn daughter approached the age that Clarissa was when she was abused, she got understandably but unhealthily protective of her girl. She cooled a relationship or two, kept her family reeled in about her, and prayed a lot. And her husband? Joe was a mite conflicted: He recognized where Clarissa was coming from, understood the intensity of her pain and her fears, had listened lovingly and empathetically when she voiced what she was feeling and why—but never did quite match the restrictiveness that Clarissa laid on their daughter. And he didn't cool a bit to the individuals Clarissa had distanced from.

Those who know them are fairly convinced that this is a tension that the family—whose kids are now grown and married—will live with for a long, long time. And they do, even (most of the time) with a measure of grace.

There are, of course, more universal transitions than abuse or the death of a child (not that these events are particularly rare): midlife crisis, crisis of faith, menopause, impotence. What transition have you observed in your spouse—or are you observing, or do you anticipate observing? A passage being endured by your beloved that touches you only because you are married? What may lurk in the personal history of your husband or wife that may thrust him/her into a singular, inner journey? What, if anything, can you do to prepare your spouse for this?

To prepare *you* for this? Use the space below to summarize your beginning place for this lesson. We'll start here and then go deeper.

read at the gate of a man's castle, his helpmate waits

From *Loving Your Husband: Building an Intimate Marriage in a Fallen World*, by Cynthia Heald[1]

"A man's house is his fortress in a warring world, where a woman's hand buckles on his armor in the morning and soothes his fatigue and wounds at night." I read this observation by Frank Crane and thought that many wives would laugh at his words. Most husbands are fortunate to receive a warm greeting when they arrive home, much less any acknowledgment of their fatigue or wounds. (I speak from experience!)

With all the stress and pressures facing today's women, it's hard to think of helping anyone else—especially our husbands! I tend to view Jack as a healthy, mature adult who can take care of himself—and so I tend to forget that he needs me to be there for him. I find myself becoming complacent in taking the initiative to help and encourage him creatively. Because I have experienced the love of God in my life and I trust His plan, His goodness, and His provision for my needs, I desire to be a helper suitable to my husband and to stand guard at his fortress.

think

- Although this advice may seem dated to you, what of value does it offer your marriage?
- If you had to update these words of advice or tailor them to your marriage, how would you revise the passage? Give it a shot.
- When was the last time you were surprised by the need of your supposedly strong and resilient spouse for acknowledgment, for affirmation, for encouragement?

think (continued)

pray

read the addicted partner

From *Victim of Love? How You Can Break the Cycle of Bad Relationships*, by Tom Whiteman and Randy Petersen[2]

If you are in an addictive relationship, get out. But here's the one exception, and it's a huge one. If you are married, try as hard as you can to keep the marriage together.

You see, though I believe that relationship addicts need to stay away from the objects of their addiction, I believe even more in the sanctity of marriage. I take those vows seriously. In the wedding ceremony, we promise to be loyal "till death do us part" (or whatever they're saying nowadays). That's an oath to God and to each other. It's not "till I no longer feel fulfilled in this relationship" or "until my partner does something really bad."

I understand that we're not talking about casual divorce: "Oh, I'm bored with this one; let me try a new spouse." I understand that we're talking about emotional heath, and that's serious. This is a very tough call, but I don't know how I can say anything other than this: If you're married, you've made a commitment to stay with that marriage. . . .

If you find yourself in an addictive marriage, you need to begin a process of *detachment*. In severe cases, this might mean an actual separation, but that's not what I have in mind. (In cases of physical abuse, I do recommend immediate separation. Abuse cannot be tolerated.) I'm talking about an emotional detachment, a process of finding yourself and releasing your partner.

Ideally, this will free you both for personal growth so you can come together later on healthier terms. At the least, it will help you in your personal growth and keep you from going down the tubes of a bad relationship.

Detachment is based on the belief that each person is responsible for him or herself. We can't solve problems that aren't ours to solve, and we can't make someone else change. We adopt a policy of keeping our hands off other people's responsibilities and tending to our own areas of weakness.

When people create problems for themselves, we need to allow them to face the consequences of their actions. We allow people to be who they are. It's their responsibility to grow, mature, and develop. We in turn accept our own responsibility for personal growth.

If we can't solve a problem and we've done all we could, we learn to live with, or in spite of, that problem. Then we try to live happily, focusing heroically on what is good in our lives today and feeling grateful for that. We learn the important lesson that making the most of what we have multiplies our blessings.

think

- What is your gut response to this line of counseling for those married to spouses with one kind or another of addiction?
- According to this excerpt, what transitional decisions should you set yourself to make if you are in an addictive marriage?
- What kind of abuse does this writer say is grounds for immediate separation? What kinds of abuse does he imply are *not* grounds for immediate separation?
- What kind of a situation would compel you to follow this advice? What kind of situation would restrain you from taking this writer's recommendations?

pray

read   speak up, honey, I can't hear you
Luke 1:5-23

During the rule of Herod, King of Judea, there was a priest assigned service in the regiment of Abijah. His name was Zachariah. His wife was descended from the daughters of Aaron. Her name was Elizabeth. Together they lived honorably before God, careful in keeping to the ways of the commandments and enjoying a clear conscience before God. But they were childless because Elizabeth could never conceive, and now they were quite old.

It so happened that as Zachariah was carrying out his priestly duties before God, working the shift assigned to his regiment, it came his one turn in life to enter the sanctuary of God and burn incense. The congregation was gathered and praying outside the Temple at the hour of the incense offering. Unannounced, an angel of God appeared just to the right of the altar of incense. Zachariah was paralyzed in fear.

But the angel reassured him, "Don't fear, Zachariah. Your prayer has been heard. Elizabeth, your wife, will bear a son by you. You are to name him John. You're going to leap like a gazelle for joy, and not only you—many will delight in his birth. He'll achieve great stature with God.

"He'll drink neither wine nor beer. He'll be filled with the Holy Spirit from the moment he leaves his mother's womb. He will turn many sons and daughters of Israel back to their God. He will herald God's arrival in the style and strength of Elijah, soften the hearts of parents to children, and kindle devout understanding among hardened skeptics—he'll get the people ready for God."

Zachariah said to the angel, "Do you expect me to believe this? I'm an old man and my wife is an old woman."

But the angel said, "I am Gabriel, the sentinel of God, sent especially to bring you this glad news. But because you won't believe me, you'll be unable to say a word until the day of your son's birth. Every word I've spoken to you will come true on time—God's time."

Meanwhile, the congregation waiting for Zachariah was getting restless, wondering what was keeping him so long in the sanctuary. When he came out and couldn't speak, they knew he had seen a vision. He continued speechless and had to use sign language with the people.

When the course of his priestly assignment was completed, he went back home.

think

- Elizabeth may have been on the verge of a gestational transition herself, but what spiritual transition did Zachariah subject himself to?
- What effects do you suppose Zachariah's personal (and very quiet) passage had on Elizabeth?
- Have you ever felt that God imposed a transition of some sort on you in order to teach you something? Talk about this if you can.

pray

read   welcome to my family

From *Blue Shoe*, by Anne Lamott[3]

Mattie noticed how many secrets she kept from William, so that he wouldn't see her as someone with a lot of problems. She wanted him to see her as someone with just a few pieces of colorful carry-on luggage, instead of multiple body bags requiring special cargo fees and handling. What if he found out she'd been sleeping with Nicky until he'd come along? What if he found out about her father, drinking with Abby on the beach? What if he found out that her mother's mind was dissolving, and that she could no longer take care of herself?

"This is home for me, Angela," Mattie said on the phone. "I've held my breath my whole life, waiting for the other shoe to drop."

There was a silence. "God only has one shoe," Angela told her.

✳ ✳ ✳

Things could have been a lot worse. Isa had a second glass of wine and got too loud but not obstreperous. Lewis fell asleep briefly in his chair and started to snore. Ella had a stomachache, and spent twenty minutes on the toilet, straining, grunting, mooing with discomfort. At least she did not need Mattie to keep her company. From Harry's closed door came the steady thud of something being thrown against the wall, a black hole pulsing. Al and Isa got into a tiff about Al's weight, which was undeniably on the rise. Mattie endured. She did not drink much, and looked over at William now and then to see what he was making of her family: Al and Isa quibbling, Lewis snoring softly, the rhythmic Edgar Allan Poe thumps from Harry's room, Ella's terrible trumpeting from the bathroom. William seemed fine. This is my beautiful screwed-up family, Mattie thought, and now you have met them all.

think

- Trace your own journey, if you can, from shielding your "beautiful screwed-up family" from friends or loved ones to becoming comfortable and less ashamed of them.
- If you've ever walked this road, what was your spouse's reaction to your gradual process of accepting your family for who they are, warts and all?
- Are you the one observing your spouse take this journey? What, if anything, can you do to lighten the load and help your spouse arrive at his or her destination in peace?

pray

read functionality

From "Readers Write: Gambling," in *The Sun* (December 2006)[4]

My husband and I have been married for twelve years. He is seventy-five; I am fifty. When I met him, I'd been through decades of abuse at the hands of a volatile mother, an absent father, and the inevitable controlling men who'd followed. He gave me peace and the strength to get the counseling and mediation I needed. We had a happy marriage.

When he entered his seventies, though, the passion went away. We tried Viagra. . . . In the meantime I preoccupied myself with work and family.

The day I met Charles was like any other. He came to my place of business to give me a quote for a job. (His wife, of all people, had referred him to me.) His tall frame, gray hair, and blue eyes sent my imagination into overdrive. After that first meeting, I was torn between my sense of loyalty to my husband and a yearning to feel a younger, stronger, fully functioning body close to mine.

One day Charles called, and I confessed everything: how much I wanted him, how I'd agonized over betraying my husband. I had no idea what his response would be. I did not know his marriage was ending.

Being touched at fifty is different from being touched at twenty, or thirty, or forty. At fifty you know your life is passing, your body is changing, and this could be your last chance.

Every time I meet my lover, I take a risk. I am amazed I can lie to my husband so easily about where I'm going or where I've been. I tell myself I'm protecting him, and that my betrayal enables me to stay in the marriage. And I will stay. I will not desert him. He will be secure in the knowledge that he is loved and respected.

Every night I say a prayer of thanks that I've made it through another day and nobody got hurt.

think

- How common do you think the writer's fiftyish dilemma is?
- How common do you think her solution is?
- What risks are you taking—with your spouse, with your kids, at your job (any of which affect your marriage)—about which, at the end of the day, you're just glad nobody got hurt?
- When was the last time you were torn between a sense of loyalty and a yearning? How did you transition through it? Are you still in it?

pray

read breakdown

From *Divine Secrets of the Ya-Ya Sisterhood*, by Rebecca Wells[5]

Vivi's body was so tense you could see the veins in her face. That's when I decided to call Beau Poché, yall's baby doctor—you probably remember him. I had no idea where your father was. Shep was never home. . . .

Beau was at the house within thirty minutes. Vivi was on the hall floor, naked underneath the robe I threw on top of her. She could not tell Beau what year it was. She could not tell him her name. He gave her a shot—some kind of tranquilizer, and she didn't fight it. A truck pulled into the driveway. I signaled to Beau that I'd go see who it was.

It was dark by then. I met your father just as he was climbing out of his truck. "Shep," I said, "Vivi's sick. She's cracked up. We've got to get her some help."

"Where are my children?" he said, angry. "Are they okay?"

"With Buggy," I said.

He turned his back, took a step toward his truck.

"Don't you even think about getting back in that truck," I told him.

Your father covered his eyes with his hands.

"Where is Vivi?" he said.

"Inside with Beau Poché."

"You called that man out to my house?"

"Yes, I did, Shep, and I don't want to hear one word about it."

"She could just be behaving actressy, Caro," he said. "You know how Vivi can be."

When your father walked into the house, he ignored Beau Poché. He spoke to Vivi.

"Vivi, Babe," he said, "you look like you could use a good meal. How bout I fix you a little something to eat?"

Then your father went into the kitchen and fried a pound of bacon. Your mother followed him in there. She sat on the floor by the stove and stared at his feet. I stood there and watched your father fry bacon, slice tomatoes, tear lettuce, and toast bread. I sat at the kitchen counter and watched him get down on the floor next to your mother and try to make her take a bite of the sandwich he'd just made. She could not remember how to chew. The food fell out of her mouth.

Shep looked up at us sitting there at the counter on those rattan stools. "Can't either of yall get my wife to take a bite of this bacon, lettuce, and tomato sandwich?" he asked, tears streaming down his face.

"No, Shep," Beau Poché said. "I'm afraid we can't."

Then your daddy picked the bacon off Vivi's lap and wiped the mayonnaise off her face. . . .

The next day Chick drove Teensy, Shep, your mama, and me to a private clinic outside New Orleans. Necie took care of yall. It was a long day. At the hospital, we wanted Vivi to sign herself in. Shep did not want her to feel like she was being put away.

But when the administrator asked Vivi what her name was, she said, "Queen Dancing Creek."

The man looked at your father.

"Ask her one more time," Shep said.

The man asked again.

"Rita Abbot Hayworth," Vivi said, "love child of H. G. Wells and Sarah Bernhardt."

I would have laughed if your mama hadn't accompanied that comment by picking up a paperweight from the administrator's desk, and throwing it so it barely missed his head. Right away, Chick put his arms around Vivi like he was hugging her. Really, he was trying to constrain her because we had no idea what she would do next.

"I'm afraid if your wife cannot give me her legal name," the man said, "this will have to be an involuntary commitment."

Your father stepped up to the man. "Listen to me, Nimrod," he said. "I'm paying the bill in this . . . joint, and if my wife wants to sign herself in as the President of the . . . United States, that's how you'll do it, you hear me? *Her name is Rita Abbott Hayworth.*

My wife signs in however she wants, and then you take . . . good care of her. She is a precious woman. Am I clear?"

Man, was he clear.

Your father kissed Vivi on the forehead before we left her. Then he cried all the way to the Monteleone Hotel, got smashed in silence, and passed out before we even ordered dinner.

think

- What is Shep's automatic response to his wife's breakdown?
- By the end of this passage, what's your evaluation of Shep's response to this crisis in his wife?
- Granted, a psychological breakdown is not your everyday marital occurrence. Still, what transition in your spouse has made you feel (if only momentarily) like fleeing rather than helping?

pray

lesson **FOUR**: the partner's transition **87**

LIVE

what i want to discuss
What have you discovered this week that you definitely want to discuss with your small group? Write that here. Then begin your small-group discussion with these thoughts.

so what?
Use the following space to summarize what you've discovered during this chapter about being married to someone trying to navigate his or her way through a personal transition. Review your Beginning Place if you need to remember where you began. How does God's truth impact the next step in your journey?

then what?
What is one practical thing you can do to apply what you've discovered? Describe how you will put this into practice. What steps will you take? Remember to think realistically; an admirable but unreachable goal is as good as no goal. Discuss your goal with your small group to further define it.

how?
Identify how you will be held accountable to the goal you described. Who will be on your support team? What are their responsibilities? How will you measure the success of your plan? Write the details here.

lesson 5

the predictable transition

You know this passage is coming, by virtue of simply being human or by being raised in your culture. You can prepare specifically for this transition, be it the birth of your first child, job change, menopause, empty nest.

the beginning place

Fairies are commonly seen or sensed, say the wise women of other times and other cultures, along creek banks and the reedy shores of ponds, and at twilight. Brownies and gremlins, sylphs and sprites, dwell along the margins of place and time, in the in-betweens, where day becomes night, where shore becomes stream, where sleeping becomes waking.

There are transitions in your life that are as common and predictable as the riverbank and twilight. Adolescence is one of them, when humans are in-between, neither entirely adults nor entirely children. There are also known, predictable transitions in the life of your marriage. Settling into monogamy, for example—that passage when the pure excitement of living together begins leveling out, when you both start sleeping in pajamas again, when you think you now know every detail about your spouse and are ready to get to know other people again.

Alas, whatever torrid passion ignited your first days or months together inevitably, predictably, tragically, or thankfully cools off into—well, into any one of a number of conditions, most of them of your choosing. What you choose may not be predictable, but the passing from sizzling romance into something else—that passage is predictable.

So is the seismic shift that occurs when children invade your marriage. Again, how you respond to this transition will determine lots about where your marriage takes you and where life will take your children. But that modulation in your marriage—that adjusting to an additional albeit tiny person in your family—is most likely on your horizon, if not already in your recent history.

That child's adolescence may be her own transition, but it will have palpable effects on your marriage, as will menopause, and retirement. Like the year's spring-to-winter cycle, some transitions in our culture are pretty near universal, and you can count on entering them sooner or later.

> The moon keeps track of the seasons,
>   the sun is in charge of each day.
> When it's dark and night takes over,
>   all the forest creatures come out.
> The young lions roar for their prey,
>   clamoring to G<small>OD</small> for their supper.
> When the sun comes up, they vanish,
>   lazily stretched out in their dens.
> Meanwhile, men and women go out to work,
>   busy at their jobs until evening.
>   —P<small>SALM</small> 104:19-23

So what transitions to come in your marriage can you see on the horizon? What marital or marriage-affecting transitions have you already passed through that you saw coming? To what extent did you prepare for them? To what extent are you preparing for predictable transitions to come? Does whatever prep you do take the form of reading, or talking to friends, or recalling how your parents did it?

Use the space below to summarize your beginning place for this lesson. We'll start here and then go deeper.

read   passionate or comfortable?

From the *National Geographic* article "Love," by Lauren Slater[1]

We are no longer beginning, my husband and I. This does not surprise me. Even back then, wearing the décor of desire, the serpentining [henna] tattoos, I knew they would fade, their red-clay color bleaching out until they were gone. On my wedding day I didn't care.

I do now. Eight years later, pale as a pillowcase, here I sit, with all the extra pounds and baggage time brings. And the questions have only grown more insistent. Does passion necessarily diminish over time? How reliable is romantic love, really, as a means of choosing one's mate? Can a marriage be good when Eros is replaced with friendship, or even economic partnership, two people bound by bank accounts?

Let me be clear: I still love my husband. There is no man I desire more. But it's hard to sustain romance in the crumb-filled quotidian that has become our lives. The ties that bind have been frayed by money and mortgages and children, those little imps who somehow manage to tighten the knot while weakening its actual fibers. Benjamin and I have no time for chilled white wine and salmon. The baths in our house always include Big Bird.

If all this sounds miserable, it isn't. My marriage is like a piece of comfortable clothing; even the arguments have a feel of fuzziness to them, something so familiar it can only be called home. And yet . . .

Renu was born into a traditional Indian family where an arranged marriage was expected. She was not an arranged kind of person, though, emerging from her earliest days as a fierce tennis player, too sweaty for saris, and smarter than many of the men around her. Nevertheless, at the age of 17, she was married off to a first cousin, a man she barely knew, a man she wanted to learn to love, but couldn't. Renu considers many arranged marriages to be acts of "state-sanctioned rape."

Renu hoped to fall in love with her husband, but the more

years that passed, the less love she felt, until, at the end she was shrunken, bitter, hiding behind the curtains of her in-laws' bungalow, looking with longing at the couple on the balcony across from theirs. "It was so obvious to me that couple had married for love, and I envied them. I really did. It hurt me so much to see how they stood together, how they went shopping for bread and eggs."

Exhausted from being forced into confinement, from being swaddled in saris that made it difficult to move, from resisting the pressure to eat off her husband's plate, Renu did what traditional Indian culture forbids one to do. She left. By this time she had had two children. She took them with her. . . .

Renu was lucky in the end. In Mumbai she met a man named Anil, and it was then, for the first time, that she felt passion. "When I first met Anil, it was like nothing I'd ever experienced. He was the first man I ever had an orgasm with. I was high, just high, all the time. And I knew it wouldn't last, couldn't last, and so that infused it with a sweet sense of longing, almost as though we were watching the end approach while we were also discovering each other."

When Renu speaks of the end, she does not, to be sure, mean the end of her relationship with Anil; she means the end of a certain stage. The two are still happily married, companionable, loving if not "in love," with a playful black dachshund they bought together. Their relationship, once so full of fire, now seems to simmer along at an even temperature, enough to keep them well fed and warm. They are grateful.

"Would I want all that passion back?" Renu asks. "Sometimes, yes. But to tell you the truth, it was exhausting."

From a physiological point of view, this couple has moved from the dopamine-drenched state of romantic love to the relative quiet of an oxytocin-induced attachment. Oxytocin is a hormone that promotes a feeling of connection, bonding. It is released when we hug our long-term spouses, or our children. It is released when a mother nurses her infant. Prairie voles, animals with high levels of oxytocin, mate for life. When scientists block oxytocin receptors in these rodents, the animals don't form monogamous bonds and tend to roam. Some researchers speculate that autism, a disorder marked by a profound inability to forge and maintain social connections, is linked to an oxytocin deficiency. Scientists have been experimenting by treating autistic people with oxytocin, which in some cases has helped alleviate their symptoms.

In long-term relationships that work — like Renu and Anil's — oxytocin is believed to be abundant in both partners. In long-term relationships that never get off the ground, like Renu and her first husband's, or that crumble once the high is gone, chances are the couple has not found a way to stimulate or sustain oxytocin production.

"But there are things you can do to help it along," says Helen Fisher [anthropologist, Rutgers University professor, and researcher of the biochemical pathways of love]. "Massage. Make love. These things trigger oxytocin and thus make you feel much closer to your partner."

Well, I suppose that's good advice, but it's based on the assumption that you still want to have sex with that boring windbag of a husband. Should you fake-it-till-you-make-it?

"Yes," says Fisher. "Assuming a fairly healthy relationship, if you have enough orgasms with your partner, you may become attached to him or her. You will stimulate oxytocin."

This may be true. But it sounds unpleasant. It's exactly what your mother always said about vegetables: "Keep eating your peas. They are an acquired taste. Eventually, you will come to like them."

But I have never been a peas person.

think

- Are you the kind of person who, by willpower and repetition, can create the feeling you want, or are you the kind who must feel a spark of enthusiasm or affection before you can pursue a feeling?

- How fair is the writer's evaluation of children as "little imps who somehow manage to tighten the knot while weakening its actual fibers"? Talk about this.
- What to you is the difference between a passionate marriage and a comfortable marriage? *Should* there be a difference? Is one a more desirable goal than the other?
- Where do dopamine and oxytocin intersect with vows and faithfulness? Do you feel that morality is a check on hormones, or that hormones reinforce morality? Or _____?

pray

read   where'd that boy go this time?

Luke 2:41-52

Every year Jesus' parents traveled to Jerusalem for the Feast of Passover. When he was twelve years old, they went up as they always did for the Feast. When it was over and they left for home, the child Jesus stayed behind in Jerusalem, but his parents didn't know it. Thinking he was somewhere in the company of pilgrims, they journeyed for a whole day and then began looking for him among relatives and neighbors. When they didn't find him, they went back to Jerusalem looking for him.

The next day they found him in the Temple seated among the teachers, listening to them and asking questions. The teachers were all quite taken with him, impressed with the sharpness of his answers. But his parents were not impressed; they were upset and hurt.

His mother said, "Young man, why have you done this to us? Your father and I have been half out of our minds looking for you."

He said, "Why were you looking for me? Didn't you know that I had to be here, dealing with the things of my Father?" But they had no idea what he was talking about.

So he went back to Nazareth with them, and lived obediently with them. His mother held these things dearly, deep within herself. And Jesus matured, growing up in both body and spirit, blessed by both God and people.

think

- So even Jesus skipped out on his parents—for at least an entire day, frightening Mary and Joseph to death. Has your child subjected you to this yet? If so, what were the circumstances?

- How are you preparing for the gradual departure of your children from your home? If the kids have already left, how'd it go?
- What good examples are there around you, among people you know, of parents who ease their kids out of the home and into independence? What nightmare scenarios do you know of?
- How do you picture living with your spouse one day with no kids in the house—just the two of you? Does the thought make you a little nervous or a little giddy?

pray

read   the big move

Genesis 31:4-7,14-18,21

So Jacob sent word for Rachel and Leah to meet him out in the field where his flocks were. He said, "I notice that your father has changed toward me; he doesn't treat me the same as before. But the God of my father hasn't changed; he's still with me. You know how hard I've worked for your father. Still, your father has cheated me over and over, changing my wages time and again. But God never let him really hurt me." . . .

Rachel and Leah said, "Has he treated us any better? Aren't we treated worse than outsiders? All he wanted was the money he got from selling us, and he's spent all that. Any wealth that God has seen fit to return to us from our father is justly ours and our children's. Go ahead. Do what God told you."

Jacob did it. He put his children and his wives on camels and gathered all his livestock and everything he had gotten, everything acquired in Paddan Aram, to go back home to his father Isaac in the land of Canaan. . . .

Jacob got away with everything he had and was soon across the Euphrates headed for the hill country of Gilead.

think

- Recall a big move you made. How did it affect your marriage?
- Have any of your big moves been colored by hurt feelings, as was the move of Jacob and his family? Worse, by hurt feelings among members of your extended family?
- How clearly (if at all) did you hear the voice of God about the reasons or circumstances of a big move? How did you feel about what you heard or didn't hear?
- What would you tell an engaged couple about the inevitability of a big move in a marriage?

lesson FIVE: the predictable transition   99

think (continued)

pray

read blended families, or colliding clans?

From *Becoming a Couple of Promise*, by Kevin Leman[2]

Truth or Myth?

_____ 1. Our new family will be much like our previous families.

_____ 2. It's easier to blend with older kids than with younger kids.

_____ 3. An older boy will be relieved when he realizes he no longer has to be "man of the house" for newly remarried Mom.

_____ 4. An older girl will probably enjoy having a new mom to serve as her role model.

_____ 5. Children usually want to call their new parent "Mom" or "Dad."

_____ 6. The younger kids appreciate having new sibling playmates added to their family.

_____ 7. Things will go more smoothly if each parent firmly disciplines the spouse's children right from the beginning.

_____ 8. When it's time for the families to merge, it's best to live in the bigger of the two adults' houses (while selling the smaller one).

_____ 9. In a blended family, the teenagers are likely to wait much longer before leaving home to start their own adult lives.

_____ 10. It's best to bring your potential spouse home early and often, so the kids can start getting used to him or her.

_____ 11. Anger is the least likely emotion to arise when blending a family.

_____ 12. Whether you respect them or not, you *do* have to love the children of your spouse.

Answers:

They are all myths! (With regard to number 1, remember that you cannot replicate your original family, even if it was a great one. Regarding number 2: In fact, a lot of older kids *resent* the fact Mom or Dad would even think about remarriage.)

think

- Blending families in a remarriage is a common marital transition these days. So, how'd you score?
- Which of the writer's opinions do you most strongly agree with? Why?
- Which do you most strongly *disagree* with? Why?
- If you've had experience in a blended family, whether as a child or a parent, what has your experience taught you about doing this transition in a healthy way?

pray

read   AARP calling . . .

From W. H. Auden, in "Sunbeams," in *The Sun*, November 2006[3]

> A tremendous number of people in America work very hard at something that bores them. Even a rich man thinks he has to go down to the office every day. Not because he likes it, but because he can't think of anything else to do.

think

- What is your first response to the idea of retiring, of not working?
- Do you feel you're the type of person who will always need the stimulation of work, whether for pay or as a volunteer?
- How will your retirement affect your marriage? How will your marriage affect your retirement?

pray

read the brush of a toe can say all that?

From "Crusoe," by George Bilgere, in *The Good Kiss*[4]

> When you've been away from it long enough
> You begin to forget the country
> Of couples, with all its customs
> And mysterious ways. Those two
> Over there, for instance: late thirties,
> Attractive and well-dressed, reading
> At the table, drinking some complicated
> Coffee drink. They haven't spoken
> Or even looked at each other in thirty minutes
>
> But the big toe of her right foot, naked
> In its sandal, sometimes grazes
> The naked ankle bone of his left foot,
>
> The faintest signal, a line thrown
>
> Between two vessels as they cruise
> Through this hour, this vacation, this life,
> Through the thick novels they're reading,
> Her toe saying to his ankle,
>
> Here's to the whole improbable story
> Of our meeting, of our life together
> And the oceanic richness
> Of our mingled narrative
> With its complex past, with its hurts
> And secret jokes, its dark closets
> And delightful sexual quirks,
> Its occasional doldrums, its vast
> Future we have already peopled
> With children. How safe we are
>
> Compared to that man sitting across the room,
> Marooned with his drink
> And yellow notebook, trying to write
> A way off his little island.

think

- If you have been married for a decade or more, what between your spouse and you is a "faintest signal, a line thrown / Between two vessels as they cruise"? What are your silent ways of communicating nothing in particular, just comfortableness with each other?
- If you are only recently married, is such silent communication among older couples a goal for you to strive for, or something to avoid?
- How inevitable do you feel it is for couples to grow into this kind of silent connecting that carries so much meaning?

pray

LIVE

what i want to discuss

What have you discovered this week that you definitely want to discuss with your small group? Write that here. Then begin your small-group discussion with these thoughts.

so what?

Use the following space to summarize what you've discovered during this chapter about predictable transitions in your marriage. Review your Beginning Place if you need to remember where you began. How does God's truth impact the next step in your journey?

then what?

What is one practical thing you can do to apply what you've discovered? Describe how you will put this into practice. What steps will you take? Remember to think realistically; an admirable but unreachable goal is as good as no goal. Discuss your goal with your small group to further define it.

how?

Identify how you will be held accountable to the goal you described. Who will be on your support team? What are their responsibilities? How will you measure the success of your plan? Write the details here.

lesson 6

the cultural transition

You live in a society that is itself in transition. How do you cope when your society's institutions—including marriage, its roles, and its expectations—are in transition?

the beginning place

You may walk the line maritally, legally, morally. How you conduct your life, how you nurture your marriage, how you rear your children, how you advance your business—this all may be absolutely appropriate (if not perfect) and what you consider "biblical" (or at least a wholehearted attempt at it).

Let's return to the image of this book's title: you may be seated firmly in your canoe, fixed unshakably on the slat in the stern of your craft. Yet the canoe that contains you is itself moving with the current, drifting or driving ahead. Even so, the culture in which we live and move and have our being is gliding inexorably through time; and although we may feel fixed on truth, hewing to tradition, living according to absolute truths—well, your spiritual and hereditary ancestors may have thought the same things, away back upstream, but your frame of reference farther downriver is plainly different from theirs.

Over a hundred years ago, well-meaning, God-seeking, Jesus-worshiping Christians defended the buying and selling of dark-skinned persons on the grounds that they were essentially inferior humans and all but created for physical labor, period. Therefore, misguided abolitionists who attempted to elevate African-Americans above their divinely appointed station were defying God's plan.

Within the last century, our spiritual forebears—who believed virtually everything about the Bible that we hold dear today—thundered out interdictions against movie theaters to their congregations. These weren't porn joints being preached against, but vaudeville theaters converted to moving-picture palaces. Innocuous as roller-skating rinks, you say—but even roller rinks were proscribed by many Bible Belt church leaders. (Sin on wheels!) These days, it's not the venue that we're warned against, but the content. When *Mary Poppins* or *The Passion of the Christ* is released, biblically living Christians are not only permitted but often urged by their pastors to enter the doors of cineplexes to see them.

Once upon some very historical and real times, very biblical and devout worshipers of Yahweh and Jesus believed that having multiple wives was perfectly acceptable in God's sight, that interest on a loan of money was immoral, that massacring the children of your enemies pleased God, and that women were forbidden by the Scriptures to teach, preach, or lead a church.

But the cultural canoe kept drifting downstream, until it has come to us—for whom (in most cases) electric guitars and a backbeat have become the expected accompaniment to worship, multiple wives are permitted if not encouraged (although one at a time, thank you), and official church leadership by females is gradually spreading throughout much of modern Christianity.

So where is culture now when it comes to biblical marriage? What about Christian marriage has shifted since your parents got married? What is shifting now, promising to make marriage noticeably different for your children than it is for you? How do you reconcile the Bible's teaching about marriage, about living with and loving your spouse, with the realities you live with?

lesson SIX: the cultural transition

Use the space below to summarize your beginning place for this lesson. We'll start here and then go deeper.

read   marriage myths

From the *New York Times* article "A Pop Quiz on Marriage," by Stephanie Coontz[1]

True or False?

1. Women are more eager to marry than men.
2. Men are threatened by women who are their intellectual and occupational equals, preferring to be with much younger, less accomplished women.
3. There are more long-term marriages today than in the past.
4. Americans have become much more tolerant of all sexual activity.
5. The growth in the number of couples living together and even having children without formal marriage ceremonies or licenses reflects a sharp break with centuries-old tradition.
6. Educated married women are increasingly "opting out" of work to stay home with their children.
7. Men and women who hold nontraditional views about gender roles are less likely to marry and more likely to divorce than those with traditional values.
8. Divorce rates in the 1950s were lower than at any other time in the 20th century.
9. Throughout history, philosophers and theologians have always believed that strong marital commitments form the foundation of a virtuous society.
10. American women have more positive attitudes toward marriage than Japanese women do.
11. Divorce has always been a disaster for women and children.
12. The preferred form of marriage through the ages has been between one man and one woman.
13. Born-again Christians are just as likely to divorce as more secular Americans.

Answers:

1. FALSE. From 1970 to the late 1990s, men's attitudes toward marriage became more favorable, while women's became less so. By the end of the century, more men than women said that marriage was their ideal lifestyle. And on average, men become more content with their marriages over time, while women grow less so. A majority of divorced men and women report that the wife was the one who wanted out of the marriage. A recent study of divorces that occurred after age 40 found that wives initiated two-thirds of them.

2. FALSE. The difference in the ages of men and women at first marriage has been narrowing for the past 80 years and is now at a historic low. By the end of the 1990s, 39 percent of women age 35-44 lived with younger men. Men still rate youth and good looks higher than women do when looking for a mate, but those criteria no longer outweigh all other. Men are much more likely now to seek a mate who has the same level of education and similar earnings potential. College-educated women are more likely to marry and less likely to divorce than women with less education.

3. TRUE. Although divorce rates have risen, death rates have fallen even more steeply, so that more couples will celebrate their 40th wedding anniversaries now than at any time in the past. Furthermore, the divorce rate reached its height more than 25 years ago. It has fallen by more than 25 percent since 1981.

4. FALSE. Americans are no more tolerant of consenting sexual relations between unmarried adults than in the past. But surveys show that disapproval of adultery, sexual coercion, rape and sex with minors has increased over the past 30 years and is now at a historic high. In 1889 a girl could legally consent to sex at 10, 11, or 12 in half the states and in Delaware the age of consent was 7.

There were many more prostitutes per capita in late 19th century America than there are today—resulting in a high incidence of venereal disease among respectably married women infected by their husbands.

5. **FALSE.** For the first thousand years of its existence, the church held that a marriage was valid if a couple claimed they had exchanged words of consent—even if there were no witnesses and no priest to officiate. Not until 1754 did England require issuance of a license for a marriage to be valid. Informal marriage and cohabitation were so common in early 19th-century America that one judge estimated that one-third of all children were born to couples who were not legally married.

6. **FALSE.** The likelihood that college-educated women will drop out of the labor force because of having children declined by half from 1984 to 2004. And among all mothers with children under 6, the most highly educated are the least likely to leave their jobs, with that likelihood declining with each level of educational attainment.

7. **TRICK QUESTION.** Women with nontraditional values are indeed more likely to divorce than women with traditional views, but they are also more likely to get married in the first place. As for men, those with traditional values about gender are more likely to marry than nontraditional men, but they are also more likely to divorce. We don't precisely know why this discrepancy exists, but it probably has something to do with the fact that women's views on gender are changing more rapidly than men's.

8. **FALSE.** Aside from a huge spike in divorce immediately after World War II, divorce rates in the 1950s were higher than in any previous decade aside from the Depression, and almost one in three marriages formed in the 1950s eventually ended in divorce. Divorce rates rose steadily from the 1890s through the 1960s (with a dip in the Depression and spike after World War II), soared in

the 1970s, and have fallen since 1981. Marriage rates, however, have also fallen significantly in the past 25 years.

9. FALSE. Ancient Roman philosophers and medieval theologians thought that loving your spouse too much was a form of "adultery," a betrayal of one's obligations to country or God. The ancient Greeks held that the purest form of love was between two men. In China, Confucian philosophers ranked the relationship between husband and wife as second from the bottom on their list of the most important family ties, with the father-eldest son relationship topping the list. Early Christians thought marriage was inescapably tainted by the presence of sex. According to the medieval church, virgins ranked highest in godliness, widows were second, and wives a distant third.

10. TRUE. In 2001 schoolgirls around the world were asked whether they agreed with the statement that everyone needed to marry. Three-quarters of American schoolgirls agree. But in Japan 88 percent of schoolgirls disagree.

11. FALSE. Divorce in modern America often does cause a sharp drop in the economic standard of living for women and children. But states that legalized no-fault divorce experienced an average 20-percent decline in suicide rates among married women over the following five years. And a recent study suggests that while divorce worsens the emotional well-being of 55 percent to 60 percent of children, it improves the well-being of 40 percent to 45 percent.

12. FALSE. The form of marriage that has been approved by more societies than any other through the ages has been polygamy—one man and many women. That family form is the one mentioned most often in the first five books of the Bible. In some societies, one woman could marry several men. In others, two families could forge an alliance by marrying off a son or daughter to the "ghost" of the other family's dead child. For most of history, the main impetus for marriage was getting in-laws and managing property, not love or sex.

13. TRUE. Thirty-five percent of born-again Christians in this country have divorced, almost the same as the 37 percent of atheists and agnostics who have divorced—and 23 percent of born-again Christians have divorced twice. Among Pentecostals, the divorce rate is more than 40 percent. The region with the highest divorce rate is the Bible Belt.

think

- So, how'd you score?
- What answers surprised you most? Why?
- Anything here with the potential to change how you live with your spouse?

pray

read chances are, your parents are divorced

From the *Christian Science Monitor* article "Is an Unhappy Marriage Better Than Divorce?"[2]

> One quarter of Americans between the ages of 18 and 44 have divorced parents. At least a million children a year since 1971 have come out of divorced families. Some of these young people feel unprepared for marriage, [sociologist Judith] Wallerstein says in an interview, because they lack "internal images of a relationship as it moves through the years."
>
> She emphasizes that people in unhappy marriages can have happy children. She adds, "A lot of people who divorce know what they're getting away from. But they have a very hazy notion of what they're getting into."

think

- Are your parents divorced? If so, did they divorce while you were still at home or after you left home?
- If your parents' marriage was intact at the time you left home, would you say it was unhappy? Why or why not?
- What "internal image" of a long-term relationship did you enter your own marriage with?
- How has that internal image changed from when you first married? Talk about this.

pray

read we're all pioneers these days

From *Marriage, A History: From Obedience to Intimacy, or How Love Conquered Marriage*, by Stephanie Coontz[3]

Over a period of two centuries, subtle shifts in economics, politics, and reproductive patterns gradually detached the married couple from the bedrock of institutions, laws, and customs that had encased them in rigid roles. Beneath the seeming continuities of marriage and family life, new fault lines opened up. In the late 1960s these changes began triggering a series of tremors that toppled familiar landmarks of family life and permanently altered the social landscape on which we build our lives. We are still feeling the aftershocks today.

Like it or not, today we are all pioneers, picking our way through uncharted and unstable territory. The old rules are no longer reliable guides to work out modern gender roles and build a secure foundation for marriage. Wherever it is that people want to end up in their family relations today, even if they are totally committed to creating a so-called traditional marriage, they have to get there by a different route from the past.

There are many people who claim they can provide you with a road map. But in fact, on virtually every issue concerning marriage today, most personal advice gurus and policy makers lag behind the real changes transforming marriage. My local bookstore has shelf after shelf of marital advice books. The titles range from *The Surrendered Wife* to *The Fifty-Fifty Marriage* to *Remaining Single and Loving It*. In 1995 *The Rules: Time-Tested Secrets for Capturing the Heart of Mr. Right* became an international bestseller. So did its 2002 follow-up, *The Rules for Marriage: Time-Tested Secrets for Making Your Marriage Work*—despite the fact that one of the two authors filed for divorce on the eve of its publication.

Unlike scholarly journals, mass-market advice books are rarely reviewed by experts in the field. Instead of getting tested research findings, most of the time you get what some author claims worked for him or her, or what someone thinks *might* work for you, or what some publisher's marketing department hopes *you* will think might work for you, all mixed in with "time-tested rules" that have worked in the past but no longer hold true.

think

- If it is true that you want a marriage that, at least in broad strokes, resembles your parents' marriage, how is your route to that destination different from the route your parents took to get there?
- In what ways could you say your marriage is uncharted territory? In what ways is it *charted* territory?
- What does the mountain of Christian books and tapes and broadcasts about "What Marriage Means" say to you (including, perhaps, this book)?
- What are some "time-tested rules" that you grew up with but that no longer work for you (or ever did)?

pray

read broken

From *Why Marriage Matters: Reasons to Believe in Marriage in Postmodern Society*, by Glenn T. Stanton[4]

> Broken homes. Broken promises. Broken hearts. Broken marriages. Broken ideals. Broken lives. Broken minds. Broken laws. Broken bodies. Broken societies. Broken people. Broken . . . everything is broken.
>
> What is so grievous about the current state of family in America is not that our nation is missing out on all the inestimable benefits of marriage. Certainly, this is tragic. Worse than we can imagine. As we have seen, because marriage is in steep decline, more adults are living shorter, less healthy lives. They are less happy, suffering from greater amounts and degrees of mental illness, and finding less fulfillment in their sexual lives. By these measures, *life is good for fewer adults.*
>
> Similarly, more children are growing up with serious emotional, physical, and intellectual handicaps. They are less secure, do more poorly in school, have more trouble with the law, engage in riskier sexual behaviors, conceive more babies. And their relationships with their parents are worse than they have ever been. By these measures, *the prospects for a good life are dimmer for more children than at any other time in America.*
>
> The collection of research in this book has served to demonstrate how all of these personal and societal pathologies can be placed at the feet of the slow, systematic death of marriage in our culture.
>
> *Slow* death. This is what is so grievous about the current state of marriage in America. The death of marriage is not some natural disaster beyond our control that has come upon us suddenly. It has been happening for more than forty years. It has happened right before our eyes and we have done nothing to stop it. In fact, there is very little indication that it even bothers us. At best, we have been passive observers. At worst, we have served as active facilitators.
>
> *Culpa Nostra*—*the fault is our own.*

think

- What evidence in your own immediate experience supports the writer's dire evaluation of where marriage is heading?
- What evidence in your own immediate experience contradicts the writer's opinion?
- What of your parents' and grandparents' marriages do you know that would match or not match with the conclusions of this passage?
- How do words like those found in the excerpt affect how you raise your own children into adolescence and beyond?

pray

read and how differently will your children do things?

From the *Washington Post* article "More Couples Choose to Wed Their Way," by Daniel de Vise[5]

> John Zielke and Jessica Briddle of Alexandria [Va.] asked the groom's father to read the vows at their wedding, held June 24 at Top of the Town in Arlington. She's a public relations consultant. He's launching a bicycle taxi service. Like many couples today, they are only vaguely religious.
>
> "I think he's a Lutheran, and I'm a Baptist, technically," Briddle said before the ceremony. "We don't attend church, so we don't have a minister, and we didn't want to be married by someone who wasn't connected to us in some way."
>
> Because the groom's father is neither a minister nor a justice of the peace, the couple plans to visit a magistrate at some point, in their jeans, to make it legal.
>
> They chose a ceremony without religious content. But they arranged for an uncle to bless the food at the reception, mostly for the sake of relatives who otherwise might have taken offense. Briddle thinks the concession "took the air out of the issue."

think

- Imagine for a moment that you and your spouse are the parents of John or Jessica. How would you respond to their plans? What would you say? How would you say it? What phone calls would you make?
- What about your wedding ceremony and reception did you feel strongly about, but about which your parents or your in-laws saw differently?
- If your grown child asked you to become temporarily certified to marry her and her beloved, would you? Talk about this.

lesson SIX: the cultural transition

think (continued)

pray

read holiness rubs off

1 Corinthians 7:12

For the rest of you who are in mixed marriages—Christian married to non-Christian—we have no explicit command from the Master. So this is what you must do. If you are a man with a wife who is not a believer but who still wants to live with you, hold on to her. If you are a woman with a husband who is not a believer but he wants to live with you, hold on to him. The unbelieving husband shares to an extent in the holiness of his wife, and the unbelieving wife is likewise touched by the holiness of her husband. Otherwise, your children would be left out; as it is, they also are included in the spiritual purposes of God.

think

- Does this teaching of St. Paul reflect his culture, or does it transcend culture? Or _____?
- How does this teaching compare with what is taught at your church? With the marital behavior of your church's members? With your own experience?
- What are the implications of the apostle's words that "we have no explicit command from the Master" about mixed marriages?

pray

LIVE

what i want to discuss

What have you discovered this week that you definitely want to discuss with your small group? Write that here. Then begin your small-group discussion with these thoughts.

so what?

Use the following space to summarize what you've discovered during this chapter about living in a culture that is itself in transition—and whose institutions, including marriage, are shifting too. Review your Beginning Place if you need to remember where you began. How does God's truth impact the next step in your journey?

then what?

What is one practical thing you can do to apply what you've discovered? Describe how you will put this into practice. What steps will you take? Remember to think realistically; an admirable but unreachable goal is as good as no goal. Discuss your goal with your small group to further define it.

how?

Identify how you will be held accountable to the goal you described. Who will be on your support team? What are their responsibilities? How will you measure the success of your plan? Write the details here.

lesson 7

the final transition

Death of marriage, death of spouse.
If it's not the end, it feels like it.

the beginning place

Granted, *final transition* is something of an oxymoron. If it's final, it's not a transition.

Yet the death of anything *feels* final—the black emptiness of a loved one's death. The death of a vision on which you've built your life, your identity, your security. The death of an intimate relationship.

Especially the death of a marriage, whether by the departure of a beloved person or by the termination of a partnership with fond memories but that went bad. The spouse left behind in the aftermath of the death or divorce typically has the roughest go (although deliberately and actively walking away from a marriage carries its own pain). Abandonment at any age is a tough transition.

Take the separation and divorce of Michael, a real-estate attorney in the Bible Belt. "Push came to shove," he remembers, "growing up in a Baptist youth group and marrying in that same church didn't give my wife much pause when she decided to walk. Not that it was a quick decision of hers—for years both of us had been depositing lots of frustrations and fears into our marriage, and when Jeanie finally saw a way out, she took it.

"She fell for a man at work, and a few months after meeting, they left together. I did a lot of crying and swearing in those days; I didn't know whether I wanted her back or wanted her dead. Dead would have been easier, I thought then—to be deprived of a wife by an accident or disease was an act of God. To be replaced by another man—this was an act of a living, choosing, sexual Jeanie. The pain of rejection and abandonment I felt just about killed me."

Michael would get some sympathy from Beryl, but not a lot. She lost her husband of fifty-plus years to cancer. It was a slow slide of a couple years from relative health to his last breath. During this time, neither Beryl nor her dying husband were any good at talking frankly about his imminent death; right before he slipped into a final coma, the two of them were still talking steadfastly, though perhaps a little forced, about what room in their house to put his bed when he came home again.

Without her beloved Robert, Beryl is a little lost in the world. You share your house and bed and fears and fetes with the same person for half a century—well, say what you want about moving on and moving beyond, but it's not easy. They nearly grew up with each other, after all—they married right out of college, and children came quickly. Whatever they learned, whatever mistakes they made, they did it together.

Beryl copes with the loneliness by remaining married to Robert—by continuing to wear her wedding band, by surrounding herself with reminders of him, by continuing to celebrate birthdays and anniversaries, if only in small and private ways, and a little sadly. More than three years later, there are still no Caribbean cruises with girlfriends, no moving into a smaller apartment—none of those major and minor gestures that, in our culture at least, signal that her grip on her departed husband is gradually relaxing. She waits for heaven now.

Transitions like these are hardly imaginable without experiencing them. For a season, it seems there is no firm ground underneath you. It is obscene to you that people around you can be birthing children and taking out the garbage and making soup and going bowling—the ongoing, mundane lives of others mock you, mock your pain.

So how close are you to the swamping white waters of this particular rapid? Been through transitions like this before? In such a stretch now? Or are you anticipating such a passage in the near or distant future? How inclined are you to prepare for such a final transition? Do you feel it's morbid to talk openly with your spouse about the possible death of your marriage or about the very likely death of one of you before the other? What examples have you seen around you, or from a distance, that are instructive about surviving such a transition? Use the space below to summarize your beginning place for this lesson. We'll start here and then go deeper.

read criticizing a king

2 Samuel 6:12-16,20-23

It was reported to King David that GOD had prospered Obed-Edom and his entire household because of the Chest of God. So David thought, "I'll get that blessing for myself," and went and brought up the Chest of God from the house of Obed-Edom to the City of David, celebrating extravagantly all the way, with frequent sacrifices of choice bulls. David, ceremonially dressed in priest's linen, danced with great abandon before GOD. The whole country was with him as he accompanied the Chest of GOD with shouts and trumpet blasts. But as the Chest of GOD came into the City of David, Michal, Saul's daughter, happened to be looking out a window. When she saw King David leaping and dancing before GOD, her heart filled with scorn. . . .

David returned home to bless his family. Michal, Saul's daughter, came out to greet him: "How wonderfully the king has distinguished himself today—exposing himself to the eyes of the servants' maids like some burlesque street dancer!" David replied to Michal, "In GOD's presence I'll dance all I want! He chose me over your father and the rest of our family and made me prince over GOD's people, over Israel. Oh yes, I'll dance to GOD's glory—more recklessly even than this. And as far as I'm concerned . . . I'll gladly look like a fool . . . but among these maids you're so worried about, I'll be honored no end."

Michal, Saul's daughter, was barren the rest of her life.

think

- These words reflect the practical death of the marriage of King David and Michal. Which words stir up your sympathy most?
- A person gets the feeling that this isn't an isolated episode, but the culmination of something. From what you know about marriage and two egos living under one roof, what *could* be the backstory here? Use your imagination.

- Do you know a marriage that is legally intact but essentially dead because of something like that between Michal and David? If you can, talk about this.

pray

read   another perfectly good night spoiled

From *A Year by the Sea: Thoughts of an Unfinished Woman*, by Joan Anderson[1]

I raise the glass to the future, just as the phone rings. Few have my number here. I consider letting it ring, but my curiosity gets the best of me. I dash for the receiver.

"Hi, it's me," my husband says. His hollow voice flattens my upbeat mood.

"Hi," I say tentatively. I've learned from several previous calls to listen hard and talk later. As the reality of our separation sinks in, he has become less friendly, more businesslike. The tenor of his voice tonight makes me uncomfortable.

"How are you doing?" he asks, a benign yet loaded question. If I say fine, and he is not fine, there will be hell to pay. I'm finding that unhappy people despise hearing good news from the contented ones. I stifle my impulse to tell him about my day, choosing to offer as little information as possible, waiting to hear the real agenda.

"The house sold," he announces matter-of-factly.

"Wow," I respond, realizing that as a couple we are now down to two homes—his and mine—with no old homestead to return to.

"We'll have some extra money," he continues. "I can rent a really nice place out here, and you can move in."

I pretend not to hear. He doesn't understand that I'm not interested in moving, period. Still, the wife in me feels obliged to offer something. "Perhaps I can visit some weekend," I reply, remaining as noncommittal as possible.

"Well, whatever," he says, backing off. Having made no specific arrangements when we parted, he probably thought after a couple of weeks I'd come to my senses and join him. The trouble is, I'm getting used to my solitude and, after a day like today, not only liking it but also seeing the worth of it.

It's not what he says that unnerves me but what he doesn't say. I have a habit of filling in blank spaces and make the grievous error of mentioning the seals.

"Seals," he says testily. "Where are they?"

"Monomoy."

"Who took you out there?"

"A fisherman friend."

"How did you meet *him*?"

No matter how I try to rescue the conversation, our moods begin to plunge. Now I'm feeling guilty and begin justifying my day, explaining more than I should. I feel strangely in his debt.

He allows that he would give anything to be wild and free, "but one of us has to be practical, after all," he says. I stifle the urge to banter further, my spirit broken. The reality of my amazing day has dissolved, the comfort of my seclusion has been disturbed. How often have I allowed someone to spoil a perfectly good mood? I struggle to breathe as I hang up. Then, in a flash, I know why I'm here. I return to the pillow on the window seat and talk to the moon.

think

- What details of this conversation reveal the awkward discomfort in a marriage that's not dead yet, but dying?
- What in this passage resonates most deeply or poignantly with you? Why?
- What proportion of hope and despair is there in this conversation for you?
- Is this snapshot of Anderson's marital history more to you an example of why a couple should hang on to their marriage, or an example of how to dissolve a marriage as neatly and with as few scars as possible?

think (continued)

pray

read working wives

From the *Social Forces* article "Women's Employment, Marital Happiness, and Divorce," by Young J. Kim[2]

> We explored the relationship between women's employment and marital disruption using data from the first and second waves of the National Survey of Families and Households. The findings did not support the role specialization hypothesis that wives' paid employment directly increases the risk of marital dissolution. Marriages in which the wife earns more than 50% of the couple's income were not more likely to dissolve. In the model without marital happiness variables, wife's employment did increase the likelihood of disruption. However, in the full model, wife's employment did not affect the risk of dissolution when both partners are happy at time 1.
>
> We found substantial support for the economic opportunity hypothesis that wives' employment is a factor in ending unhappy marriages but does not affect happy marriages. Wives' labor force participation did not increase the risk of disruption for couples in which both partners are happy at time 1. When both partners are not happy at time 1, there was a significant increase in the likelihood of disruption when the wife is employed than when the wife is not employed. The results led us to the conclusion that women's employment plays an enabling role that is important in explaining contemporary divorce patterns, but that women's employment does not destabilize marriage.

think

- In two-income marriages, what does this study conclude *isn't* the direct cause of a marital dissolution? What does it conclude *is*?
- Are your opinions about two-income marriages and wives working outside the home generally confirmed or contradicted by this research?

- Is the study's conclusion reassuring to you and your marriage, or worrisome? Why?

pray

lesson SEVEN: the final transition   **135**

read while you live, love well

From Sonnet 73, by Shakespeare[3]

> That time of year thou mayst in me behold
> When yellow leaves, or none, or few, do hang
> Upon those boughs which shake against the cold,
> Bare ruin'd choirs, where late the sweet birds sang.
> In me thou seest the twilight of such day
> As after sunset fadeth in the west,
> Which by and by black night doth take away,
> Death's second self, that seals up all in rest.
> In me thou see'st the glowing of such fire
> That on the ashes of his youth doth lie,
> As the death-bed whereon it must expire
> Consumed with that which it was nourish'd by.
> This thou perceivest, which makes thy love more strong,
> To love that well which thou must leave ere long.

think

- With what three images does the writer compare himself as he grows older?
- Does this sonnet seem to you more morbid than romantic? Why or why not?
- How do you picture yourself growing older with your spouse and anticipating the death of one of you before the other?

think (continued)

pray

lesson SEVEN: the final transition

read   ruined by the strong one

Ruth 1:1-9,16-21; 4:13-17

Once upon a time—it was back in the days when judges led Israel—there was a famine in the land. A man from Bethlehem in Judah left home to live in the country of Moab, he and his wife and his two sons. The man's name was Elimelech; his wife's name was Naomi; his sons were named Mahlon and Kilion—all Ephrathites from Bethlehem in Judah. They all went to the country of Moab and settled there.

Elimelech died and Naomi was left, she and her two sons. The sons took Moabite wives; the name of the first was Orpah, the second Ruth. They lived there in Moab for the next ten years. But then the two brothers, Mahlon and Kilion, died. Now the woman was left without either her young men or her husband.

One day she got herself together, she and her two daughters-in-law, to leave the country of Moab and set out for home; she had heard that God had been pleased to visit his people and give them food. And so she started out from the place she had been living, she and her two daughters-in-law with her, on the road back to the land of Judah.

After a short while on the road, Naomi told her two daughters-in-law, "Go back. Go home and live with your mothers. And may God treat you as graciously as you treated your deceased husbands and me. May God give each of you a new home and a new husband!" She kissed them and they cried openly. . . .

But Ruth said, "Don't force me to leave you; don't make me go home. Where you go, I go; and where you live, I'll live. Your people are my people, your God is my god; where you die, I'll die, and that's where I'll be buried, so help me God—not even death itself is going to come between us!"

When Naomi saw that Ruth had her heart set on going with her, she gave in. And so the two of them traveled on together to Bethlehem.

When they arrived in Bethlehem the whole town was soon buzzing: "Is this really our Naomi? And after all this time!"

But she said, "Don't call me Naomi; call me Bitter. The Strong One has dealt me a bitter blow. I left here full of life, and God has brought me back with nothing but the clothes on my back. Why would you call me Naomi? God certainly doesn't. The Strong One ruined me."

※ ※ ※

Boaz married Ruth. She became his wife. Boaz slept with her. By God's gracious gift she conceived and had a son.

The town women said to Naomi, "Blessed be God! He didn't leave you without family to carry on your life. May this baby grow up to be famous in Israel! He'll make you young again! He'll take care of you in old age. And this daughter-in-law who has brought him into the world and loves you so much, why, she's worth more to you than seven sons!"

Naomi took the baby and held him in her arms, cuddling him, cooing over him, waiting on him hand and foot.

The neighborhood women started calling him "Naomi's baby boy!" But his real name was Obed. Obed was the father of Jesse, and Jesse the father of David.

think

- How did Naomi reap more than her fair share of tragedy?
- Do you know or have you heard of anyone who lost what Naomi lost, or at least came close?
- What compensation comes to Naomi at the end of this narration? Does this ring more of reality or of fairy tale to you? Why?
- In the presence of someone who lost as much as Naomi lost, are you reluctant or ready to describe the biblical Naomi's eventual happiness as a way to give your friend hope? Why?

lesson SEVEN: the final transition

think (continued)

pray

read into the unknown

From *Two-Part Invention: The Story of a Marriage,* by Madeleine L'Engle[4]

Now I am setting out into the unknown. It will take me a long while to work through the grief. There are no shortcuts; it has to be gone through. . . .

A couple of years ago a friend called me from her hospital bed, demanding, "Madeleine, do you believe everything that you have written in your books?"

I said *yes* then. It is still *yes* today.

But grief still has to be worked through. It is like walking through water. Sometimes there are little waves lapping about my feet. Sometimes there is an enormous breaker that knocks me down. Sometimes there is a sudden and fierce squall. But I know that many waters cannot quench love, neither can the floods drown it.

We are not good about admitting grief, we Americans. It is embarrassing. We turn away, afraid that it might happen to us. But it is part of life, and it has to be gone through. . . .

Does a marriage end with the death of one of the partners? In a way, yes. I made my promises to Hugh "till death us do part," and that has happened. But the marriage contract is not the love that builds up over many years, and which never ends, as the circle of our wedding band never ends. Hugh will always be part of me, go with me wherever I go, and that is good because, despite our faults and flaws and failures, what we gave each other was good. I am who I am because of our years together, freed by his acceptance and love of me. . . .

When I married I opened myself to the possibility of great joy and great pain and I have known both. Hugh's death is like an amputation. But would I be willing to protect myself by having rejected marriage? By having rejected love? No. I wouldn't have missed a minute of it, not any of it.

think

- In what ways does death *not* end a marriage? Talk about this.
- What of you is you because of years together with your wife or husband?
- "We are not good about admitting grief, we Americans." Agree or disagree? Why?
- How inclined are you to ponder the death of your spouse, and your life beyond that season? If you can, talk about this.

pray

LIVE

what i want to discuss

What have you discovered this week that you definitely want to discuss with your small group? Write that here. Then begin your small-group discussion with these thoughts.

so what?

Use the following space to summarize what you've discovered during this chapter about the death of a marriage or spouse, or a similar transition that seems utterly final to you. Review your Beginning Place if you need to remember where you began. How does God's truth impact the next step in your journey?

then what?

What is one practical thing you can do to apply what you've discovered? Describe how you will put this into practice. What steps will you take? Remember to think realistically; an admirable but unreachable goal is as good as no goal. Discuss your goal with your small group to further define it.

how?

Identify how you will be held accountable to the goal you described. Who will be on your support team? What are their responsibilities? How will you measure the success of your plan? Write the details here.

lesson 8

hope for your marriage in transition

Decide where to go from here in your marriage and how to get there.

a time to review

We come to the final lesson in our *Shooting the Rapids in a Wooden Canoe* discussion guide. But this is not an ending place. With any luck (and the prayers of people who care for you), you've been discovering some truths about your life—particularly, your marriage—and have seen opportunity for change. Positive change. But no matter what has brought you to this final lesson, you know that it's only a pause in your journey.

You may have uncovered behaviors or thoughts that demanded change. Perhaps you've already changed them. Will the changes stick? How will you and your spouse continue to take the momentum from this study into next week, next month, and next year? Use your time in this lesson not only to review what you discovered but also to determine how you'll stay on track tomorrow.

You'll notice that there's a "Live" section in this lesson matched with each of the previous seven lessons. Use this to note the ongoing plans of you and your spouse. Talk about your plans with small-group members. Commit your plans to prayer. And then do what you say you'll do. As you move forward with a renewed sense of purpose, you'll become more confident learning every day how better to live with your mate for better or for worse—and with the confidence will come, gradually, more success at becoming the couple you both want to become.

lesson EIGHT: hope for your marriage in transition

read   the unexpected transition

Matthew 1:18-20,24

Joseph discovered [Mary] was pregnant. (It was by the Holy Spirit, but he didn't know that.) Joseph, chagrined but noble, determined to take care of things quietly so Mary would not be disgraced.

While he was trying to figure a way out, he had a dream. God's angel spoke in the dream: "Joseph, son of David, don't hesitate to get married." . . .

Then Joseph woke up. He did exactly what God's angel commanded in the dream: He married Mary.

think

- What of late has troubled you about your marriage?
- Besides dreams, what avenues can you imagine may bring some insight to your dilemma?

pray

LIVE

How does God's truth influence the next step you'll take with your spouse in your marriage journey?

How will you take that next step?

How will you be held accountable?

read   the cataclysmic transition

2 Samuel 12:15-20

After Nathan went home, GOD afflicted the child that Uriah's wife bore to David, and he came down sick. David prayed desperately to God for the little boy. He fasted, wouldn't go out, and slept on the floor. The elders in his family came in and tried to get him off the floor, but he wouldn't budge. Nor could they get him to eat anything. On the seventh day the child died. . . .

David noticed that the servants were whispering behind his back, and realized that the boy must have died.

He asked the servants, "Is the boy dead?"

"Yes," they answered. "He's dead."

David got up from the floor, washed his face and combed his hair, put on a fresh change of clothes, then went into the sanctuary and worshiped. Then he came home and asked for something to eat. They set it before him and he ate.

think

- What cataclysmic transition have you experienced that felt like it would kill you?
- In what sense is David's reaction to the news of his son's death a model for you if and when such a time should arrive in the life of your marriage?

pray

LIVE

How does God's truth influence the next step you'll take with your spouse in your marriage journey?

How will you take that next step?

How will you be held accountable?

read   the masked transition

Matthew 27:17-19,24

With the crowd before him, Pilate said, "Which prisoner do you want me to pardon: Jesus Barabbas, or Jesus the so-called Christ?" He knew it was through sheer spite that they had turned Jesus over to him.

While court was still in session, Pilate's wife sent him a message: "Don't get mixed up in judging this noble man. I've just been through a long and troubled night because of a dream about him." . . .

When Pilate saw that he was getting nowhere and that a riot was imminent, he took a basin of water and washed his hands in full sight of the crowd, saying, "I'm washing my hands of responsibility for this man's death. From now on, it's in your hands. You're judge and jury."

think

- Are there any slow, simmering, barely perceptible transitions in you and your spouse that are moving in different directions and that may one day come to a testing point?
- What in your marriage is the difference between growing apart and growing differently?

pray

lesson **EIGHT**: hope for your marriage in transition

LIVE

How does God's truth influence the next step you'll take with your spouse in your marriage journey?

How will you take that next step?

How will you be held accountable?

read the partner's transition

Luke 1:13,18-22

But the angel reassured him, "Don't fear, Zachariah. Your prayer has been heard. Elizabeth, your wife, will bear a son by you. You are to name him John." . . .

Zachariah said to the angel, "Do you expect me to believe this? I'm an old man and my wife is an old woman."

But the angel said, "I am Gabriel, the sentinel of God, sent especially to bring you this glad news. But because you won't believe me, you'll be unable to say a word until the day of your son's birth. Every word I've spoken to you will come true on time—God's time."

Meanwhile, the congregation waiting for Zachariah was getting restless, wondering what was keeping him so long in the sanctuary. When he came out and couldn't speak, they knew he had seen a vision. He continued speechless and had to use sign language with the people.

think

- How has a personal passage you've had to make affected your spouse? Or how has a personal passage your spouse has had to make affected you?
- What passage might one of you be in now?

pray

lesson EIGHT: hope for your marriage in transition

LIVE

How does God's truth influence the next step you'll take with your spouse in your marriage journey?

How will you take that next step?

How will you be held accountable?

read   the predictable transition

Luke 2:42-48

When he was twelve years old, they went up as they always did for the Feast. When it was over and they left for home, the child Jesus stayed behind in Jerusalem, but his parents didn't know it. Thinking he was somewhere in the company of pilgrims, they journeyed for a whole day and then began looking for him among relatives and neighbors. When they didn't find him, they went back to Jerusalem looking for him.

The next day they found him in the Temple seated among the teachers, listening to them and asking questions. The teachers were all quite taken with him, impressed with the sharpness of his answers. But his parents were not impressed; they were upset and hurt.

His mother said, "Young man, why have you done this to us? Your father and I have been half out of our minds looking for you."

think

- Where are your children in their gradual separation from parents and home?
- What are your feelings about the prospect of your child eventually living apart from you?

pray

lesson **EIGHT**: hope for your marriage in transition

LIVE

How does God's truth influence the next step you'll take with your spouse in your marriage journey?

How will you take that next step?

How will you be held accountable?

read   the cultural transition

1 Corinthians 7:12

For the rest of you who are in mixed marriages—Christian married to non-Christian—we have no explicit command from the Master. So this is what you must do. If you are a man with a wife who is not a believer but who still wants to live with you, hold on to her. If you are a woman with a husband who is not a believer but he wants to live with you, hold on to him. The unbelieving husband shares to an extent in the holiness of his wife, and the unbelieving wife is likewise touched by the holiness of her husband. Otherwise, your children would be left out; as it is, they also are included in the spiritual purposes of God.

think

- How have cultural shifts made your marriage significantly different from your parents' marriage?
- Do you have any clues about how the marriages of your children will one day differ from your marriage?

pray

LIVE

How does God's truth influence the next step you'll take with your spouse in your marriage journey?

How will you take that next step?

How will you be held accountable?

lesson EIGHT: hope for your marriage in transition

read   the final transition

Ruth 1:3-7

Elimelech died and Naomi was left, she and her two sons. The sons took Moabite wives; the name of the first was Orpah, the second Ruth. They lived there in Moab for the next ten years. But then the two brothers, Mahlon and Kilion, died. Now the woman was left without either her young men or her husband.

One day she got herself together, she and her two daughters-in-law, to leave the country of Moab and set out for home; she had heard that God had been pleased to visit his people and give them food. And so she started out from the place she had been living, she and her two daughters-in-law with her, on the road back to the land of Judah.

think

- What loss have you experienced regarding your marriage? If you haven't, what marital loss can you reasonably anticipate in the future?
- What road would it be wise for you to start out on, in response to a present or future loss of your marriage or spouse?

pray

LIVE

How does God's truth influence the next step you'll take with your spouse in your marriage journey?

How will you take that next step?

How will you be held accountable?

notes

lesson 1: the unexpected transition
1. Wendy Carlos, http://www.wendycarlos.com/open.html.
2. Richard Schwartz and Jacqueline Olds, *Marriage in Motion: The Natural Ebb and Flow of Lasting Relationships* (Cambridge, MA: Perseus, 2000), 77.
3. Anne Roiphe, *Married: A Fine Predicament* (New York: Basic Books, 2002), 110-111.
4. Barbara Kingsolver, *The Poisonwood Bible* (New York: HarperPerennial, 1998), 199-200.
5. Robert Hicks, *Uneasy Manhood* (Nashville, TN: Thomas Nelson, 1991), 57, quoted in Cynthia Hicks and Robert Hicks, *The Feminine Journey: Understanding the Biblical Stages of a Woman's Life* (Colorado Springs, CO: NavPress, 1994), 158.
6. Bill Thrall, Bruce McNicol, and John Lynch, *TrueFaced: Trust God and Others with Who You Really Are* (Colorado Springs, CO: NavPress, 2003), 28.

lesson 2: the cataclysmic transition
1. Lucy Larcom, "Sunbeams," *The Sun*, May 2004.
2. http://www.healthdiaries.com/health_quotations/archives/anton_chekhov/.
3. Anne Roiphe, *Married: A Fine Predicament* (New York: Basic Books, 2002), 185-187. Reprinted by permission of Basic Books, a member of Perseus Book Group.
4. Helge Rubinstein, ed., *The Oxford Book of Marriage* (Oxford University Press, 1990), 183.
5. Coleman Barks with John Moyne, trans., *The Essential Rumi* (Edison, NJ: Castle Books, 1995), 47-49.

6. Stuart Briscoe, *Brave Enough to Follow: What Jesus Can Do When You Keep Your Eyes on Him* (Colorado Springs, CO: NavPress, 2004), 140-141, 143.
7. Karen S. Peterson, *USA Today*, a division of Gannett Co. Inc. December 21, 1998, http://www.divorcereform.org/mel/raffairstats.html. Reprinted with permission.
8. Adam Phillips, *Monogamy* (New York: Pantheon, 1996), 2.

lesson 3: the masked transition

1. George Eliot, *Middlemarch* (London: Penguin Books, 1871-72, 1994), 652.
2. Cristina Nehring, "Of Sex and Marriage," review of *Mating in Captivity: Reconciling the Erotic and the Domestic*, by Esther Perel, *The Atlantic Monthly*, December 2006, 124-126.
3. Garrison Keillor, *Wobegon Boy* (New York: Viking, 1997), 118-119.
4. Nina Utne, "Pillow Talk: A Conversation with Stephen and Ondrea Levine About Lust, the Meaning of Marriage, and True Intimacy," *Utne*, March–April 2006, 53. Reprinted with permission from *Utne* magazine (March/April 2006); www.utne.com.
5. C. S. Lewis, *A Grief Observed* (London: Faber & Faber, 1961), 40-41.

lesson 4: the partner's transition

1. Frank Crane, in J. Allan Petersen, ed., *The Marriage Affair* (Carol Stream, IL: Tyndale, 1971), 92, quoted in Cynthia Heald, *Loving Your Husband: Building an Intimate Marriage in a Fallen World* (Colorado Springs, CO: NavPress, 1989), 35-36.
2. Tom Whiteman and Randy Petersen, *Victim of Love? How You Can Break the Cycle of Bad Relationships* (Colorado Springs, CO: Piñon Press, 1998), 200-203.
3. From *Blue Shoe* by Anne Lamott, copyright © 2002 by Anne Lamott. Used by permission of Riverhead Books, an imprint of Penguin Group (USA) Inc.
4. "Readers Write: Gambling," *The Sun*, December 2006, 36-37.
5. Selection from pages 303-304 from *Divine Secrets of the Ya-Ya Sisterhood* by Rebecca Wells. Copyright © 1996 by Rebecca Wells. Reprinted by permission of HarperCollins Publishers.

lesson 5: the predictable transition

1. Lauren Slater, "Love," *National Geographic* Image Collection, February 2006, 34-35, 45, 48.
2. Kevin Leman, *Becoming a Couple of Promise* (Colorado Springs, CO: NavPress, 1999), 158, 174.

3. W. H. Auden, "Sunbeams," *The Sun*, November 2006, 48.
4. "Crusoe," from *The Good Kiss*, The University of Akron Press, copyright 2002 by George Bilgere. Reprinted by permission of The University of Akron Press.

lesson 6: the cultural transition

1. Stephanie Coontz, "A Pop Quiz on Marriage," *New York Times*, February 18, 2006, http://www.nytimes.com/2006/02/19/opinion/19coontz.html?ex=1165986000&en=fd82d1e45b4bee23&ei=5070. © 2006 *The New York Times*. Reprinted by permission.
2. By Marlin Gardner. Excerpted with permission from the October 4, 2000 issue of *The Christian Science Monitor* (www.csmonitor.com). ©2000 *The Christian Science Monitor*. All rights reserved.
3. Stephanie Coontz, *Marriage, A History: From Obedience to Intimacy, or How Love Conquered Marriage* (New York: Viking, 2005), 282-283.
4. Glenn T. Stanton, *Why Marriage Matters: Reasons to Believe in Marriage in Postmodern Society* (Colorado Springs, CO: Piñon Press, 1997), 159-160.
5. Daniel de Vise, "More Couples Choose to Wed Their Way," *Washington Post*, July 2, 2006, C1.

lesson 7: the final transition

1. From *A Year by the Sea by* Joan Andersen, copyright © 1999 by Joan Andersen. Used by permission of Broadway Books, a division of Random House, Inc.
2. "Women's Employment, Marital Happiness, and Divorce." From *Social Forces*, vol. 81, no.2 Copyright © 2002 by the University of North Carolina Press. Used by permission of the publisher.www.unpress.unc.edu.
3. William Shakespeare, *Sonnet 73*, http://www.shakespeare-online.com/sonnets/73.html.
4. Excerpt from *Two-Part Invention: The Story of a Marriage* by Madeleine L'Engle. Copyright © 1988 by Crosswicks Ltd. Reprinted by permission of Farrar, Straus and Giroux, LLC.

MORE FROM THE REAL LIFE STUFF FOR COUPLES SERIES.

Pedaling Tandem for the Long Haul
The Navigators
ISBN-13: 978-1-60006-163-9
ISBN-10: 1-60006-163-X

Love and marriage should be spontaneous and carefree, right? While a word like "deliberate" doesn't inspire visions of romance, *Pedaling Tandem for the Long Haul* shares the value found in infusing a marriage with purpose and vision. This study seeks to wed the spontaneous with the deliberate, and keep them together until death do they part.

Running a Three-Legged Race Across Time
The Navigators
ISBN-13: 978-1-60006-018-2
ISBN-10: 1-60006-018-8

In one word, describe your marriage. If you answered anything other than "perfect," you need the honest truth from this new Bible discussion guide on staying married in a culture hostile to marriage.

Dancing the Tango in an Earthquake
The Navigators
ISBN-13: 978-1-60006-019-9
ISBN-10: 1-60006-019-6

Together with your spouse or a couples small group, read excerpts about seven major marriage distractions and how you can prevent them from clouding your view of the ultimate prize: a marriage that works.

NAVPRESS
BRINGING TRUTH TO LIFE
www.navpress.com

To order copies, visit your local Christian bookstore, call NavPress at 1-800-366-7788, or log on to www.navpress.com.
To locate a Christian bookstore near you, call 1-800-991-7747.